TALKING WITH GOD

St. Alphonsus Liguori

Alphonsus Maria de'Liguori was born in Marianella, near Naples, of noble parents in September 1696. In 1726 he entered the priesthood and later founded the missionary Congregation of the Most Holy Redeemer, popularly known as the Redemptorists. At the age of sixty-six, he was consecrated Bishop of St. Agatha.

St. Alphonsus wrote his first book at age forty-nine, and went on to author more than one hundred books on spirituality and theology over his lifetime. Many of these books were written in the half-hours snatched from his labors as missionary, religious superior, and Bishop. He died in August 1787, at age ninety-one. St. Alphonsus was beatified in 1816, canonized in 1839, and declared a Doctor of the Church in 1871.

Scriptoria Books

The word "scriptoria" literally means "places for writing." Historically, scriptoria were writing rooms; areas set apart in some monasteries for the use of scribes, or copyists of the community, to faithfully create or reproduce books by hand. Their work was exacting, and great care was taken to ensure a high degree of copy fidelity.

Scriptoria Books continues in the traditions set forth in these communities long ago. Each new Scriptoria publication has been transcribed word for word from an original text, then edited, formatted, typeset, and proofread through each revision. Our procedures are not automated. Our books are not facsimiles; they are carefully created new editions of classic works.

TALKING
WITH
GOD

*Four Treatises on the Interior Life
from St. Alphonsus Liguori*

- The Way to Converse with God
- A Short Treatise on Prayer
- Mental Prayer
- The Presence of God

St. Alphonsus Liguori

Doctor of the Church

Bishop of St. Agatha, and Founder of the
Congregation of the Most Holy Redeemer

Scriptoria Books

Talking with God: Four Treatises on the Interior Life
from St. Alphonsus Liguori

Copyright © 2011

Talking with God : Four Treatises on the Interior Life
from St. Alphonsus Liguori ; The Way to Converse
Always and Familiarly with God , A Short Treatise on
Prayer , Mental Prayer , The Presence of God / by St.
Alphonsus Liguori.
p. cm.
Includes bibliographical references.
ISBN 9780615516370 (pbk)
1. Prayer. 2. Spiritual Life.
I. Liguori, Alphonsus, Saint (1696-1787).

Printed in the United States of America

Scriptoria Books
Mesa, Arizona, USA

www.scriptoriabooks.com

NOTICE

All Biblical citations in this edition are from the Latin Vulgate. English translations of Bible texts are derived from the Douay-Rheims Bible. Direct correlation of these citations with other versions of the Bible may be problematic, due to differences in enumeration, nomenclature, and content between the various editions. — ED

CONTENTS

THE WAY TO CONVERSE ALWAYS AND FAMILIARLY WITH GOD

I.	God Wishes Us to Speak to Him	3
II.	It is Easy and Agreeable .	8
III.	Of What, When, and How	
	1. In General	12
	2. In Trials	13
	3. In Joys.	17
	4. After a Fault	18
	5. In Doubts	21
	6. For Your Neighbor	22
	7. The Desire for Heaven	22
IV.	God Answers the Soul That Speaks to Him	24
V.	Practical Summary	25

A SHORT TREATISE ON PRAYER

I.	The Necessity of Prayer .	37
II.	The Efficacy of Prayer	41
III.	The Conditions Required for Prayer	
	1. Humility .	45
	2. Confidence	46
	3. Perseverance .	48
IV.	God Hears the Prayers of Sinners	52
V.	God Has Pledged to Grant Us Spiritual Goods	55
VI.	Conclusion	60
	Prayer .	62

MENTAL PRAYER

I.	Morally Necessary for Salvation	
	1. It Enlightens the Mind	65
	2. It Disposes the Heart to Practice Virtues	67
	3. It Helps Us to Pray as We Should	70

II.	Indispensable to Attain Perfection	73
	Prayer	78
III.	The Ends of Mental Prayer	
	1. To Unite Ourselves to God	79
	2. To Obtain Grace from God	81
	3. Not to Seek Spiritual Consolations	83
IV.	Principal Subjects of Meditation	85
V.	The Place and the Time Suitable for Meditation	
	1. The Place	87
	2. The Time	89
VI.	Manner of Making Mental Prayer	
	1. The Preparation	93
	2. The Meditation	95
	3. The Conclusion	102
VII.	Distractions and Aridities	
	1. Distractions	104
	2. Aridities	105
	Prayer	108

THE PRESENCE OF GOD

I.	Effects Produced by This Holy Exercise	
	1. The Avoidance of Sin	111
	2. The Practice of Virtue	115
	3. To Unite the Soul with God	116
II.	Practice of the Presence of God	
	Of the Intellect	
	1. Imagine Christ is Present	118
	2. Beholding with Eyes of Faith	119
	3. Recognize Him in His Creatures	121
	4. Consider God within Us	123
	Of the Will	
	1. Frequently Raising the Heart to God . . .	129
	2. The Intention of Pleasing God	132
	3. Recollect Yourself with God	133
	Prayer	135

EDITOR'S PREFACE

This book contains four works, of St. Alphonsus Liguori, detailing the mysteries of the interior life. Although this modest collection is but a small portion of his numerous treatises, they reveal the spirit, the heart, and the talent of St. Alphonsus, as he poured out his soul in his writings.

The treatises of St. Alphonsus are not works created for the purpose of exercising the mind; his writings are intended to nourish, and they are destined to give strength to the life of the soul. Readers are encouraged to take daily, the amount that is most appropriate for their own spiritual temperament. — ED*.

---

*Reverend Eugene Grimm, C.Ss.R, Editor of *The Complete Ascetical Works of St. Alphonsus de Liguori*, v. 2., Notice, p. 5.

THE WAY TO CONVERSE ALWAYS
AND FAMILIARLY WITH GOD

THE WAY TO CONVERSE ALWAYS AND FAMILIARLY WITH GOD

I

God Wishes Us to Speak to Him

HOLY Job was struck with wonder to consider our God so devoted in benefiting man, and showing the chief care of his heart to be, to love man and to make himself beloved by him. Speaking to the Lord, he exclaims, *What is man, that You should magnify him, or why do You set Your Heart upon him?* (Job 7:17). Hence it is clearly a mistake to think that great confidence and familiarity in treating with God is a want of reverence to his Infinite Majesty. You ought indeed, O devout soul! to revere him in all humility, and abase yourself before him; especially when you call to mind the unthankfulness and the outrages whereof, in past times, you have been guilty. Yet this should not hinder your treating with him with the most tender love and confidence in your power. He is Infinite Majesty; but at the same time he is Infinite Goodness, Infinite Love. In God you possess the

3

Lord most exalted and supreme; but you have also him who loves you with the greatest possible love. He disdains not, but delights that you should use towards him that confidence, that freedom and tenderness, which children use towards their mothers. Hear how he invites us to come to his feet, and the caresses he promises to bestow on us: *You shall be carried at the breasts, and upon the knees they shall caress you: as one whom the mother caresses, so will I comfort you* (Isa. 66:12). As a mother delights to place her little child upon her knees, and so to feed or to caress him; with like tenderness does our gracious God delight to treat the souls whom he loves, who have given themselves wholly to him, and placed all their hopes in his goodness.

Consider, you have no friend nor brother, nor father nor mother, nor spouse nor lover, who loves you more than your God. The divine grace is that great treasure whereby we vilest of creatures, we servants, become the dear friends of our Creator himself: *For she is an infinite treasure to men, which they that use, become the friends of God* (Wis. 7:14). For this purpose he increases our confidence; he *emptied himself* (Phil. 2:7), and brought himself to nothing, so to speak; abasing himself even to becoming man and conversing familiarly with us: *He conversed with men* (Bar. 3:38). He went so far as to become an infant, to

4

become poor, even so far as openly to die the death of a malefactor upon the cross. He went yet farther, even to hide himself under the appearance of bread, in order to become our constant companion and unite himself intimately to us: *He that eats My Flesh and drinks My Blood abides in Me, and I in him* (John 6:57). In a word, he loves you as much as though he had no love but towards yourself alone. For which reason you ought to have no love for any but for himself. Of him, therefore, you may say, and you ought to say, *My Beloved to me, and I to Him* (Cant. 2:16). My God has given himself all to me, and I give myself all to him; He has chosen me for his beloved, and I choose him, of all others, for my only Love: *My Beloved is white and ruddy, chosen out of thousands* (Cant. 5:10).

Say, then, to him often, O my Lord! why do You love me so? what good thing do You see in me? Have You forgotten the injuries I have done You? But since You have treated me so lovingly, and instead of casting me into hell, have granted me so many favors, whom can I desire to love from this day forward but You, my God, my all? Ah, most gracious God, if in time past I have offended You, it is not so much the punishment I have deserved that now grieves me, as the displeasure I have given You, who are worthy of infinite love. But You know not how to despise a heart that repents and humbles itself: *A contrite and humble heart, O God, You will not despise* (Ps. 50:19). Ah, now, indeed, neither in this life nor in the other do I desire any but You alone: *What have I in heaven? and besides You what do I desire upon earth! You are the God of my heart, and the God that is my portion forever* (Ps. 72:25). You alone are and shall be forever the only Lord of my heart, of my will; You my only good, my heaven, my hope, my love, my all: "The God of my heart, and the God that is my portion forever."

The more to strengthen your confidence in God, often call to mind his loving treatment of you, and the gracious means he has used to drive you from the disorders of your life and your attachments to earth, in order to draw you to his holy love; and therefore fear to have too little confidence in treating [*dealing*] with your God, now that you have a resolute will to love and to please him with all your power. The mercies he has granted you are most sure pledges of the love he bears you. God is displeased with a want of trust on the part of souls that heartily love him, and whom he loves. If, then, you desire to please his loving heart, converse with him from this day forward with the greatest confidence and tenderness you can possibly have.

I have graven you in My hands: your walls are always before My eyes (Isa. 49:16). Beloved soul, says the Lord, what do you fear or mistrust? I have you written in my hands, so as never to forget to do you good. Are you afraid of your enemies? Know that the care of your defense is always before me, so that I cannot lose sight of it. Therefore did David rejoice, saying to God, *You have crowned us as with a shield of Your good will* (Ps. 5:13). Who, O Lord! can ever harm us, if You with Your goodness and love do defend and encompass us round about? Above all, animate your confidence at the thought of the gift that God has given us of Jesus Christ: *God so loved the world as to give His only begotten Son* (John 3:16). How can we ever fear, exclaims the Apostle, that God would refuse us any good, after he has granted to give us his own Son? *He delivered Him up for us all; how has He not also, with Him, given us all things?* (Rom. 8:32).

My delights are to be with the children of men (Prov. 8:31). The paradise of God, so to speak, is the heart of man. Does God love you? Love him. His delights are to be with you; let yours be to be with himself, to pass all your lifetime with him, in the delight of whose company you hope to spend a blissful eternity. Accustom yourself to speak with him alone, familiarly, with confidence and love, as to the dearest friend you have, and who loves you best.

II

It is Easy and Agreeable

IF it be a great mistake, as has been already said, to converse mistrustfully with God — to be always coming before him as a slave, full of fear and confusion, comes before his prince, trembling with dread — it would be a greater to think that conversing with God is but weariness and bitterness. No, it is not so: *Her conversation has no bitterness, nor her company any tediousness* (Wis. 8:16). Ask those souls who love him with a true love, and they will tell you that in the sorrows of their life they find no greater, no truer relief, than in a loving converse with God.

Now this does not require that you continually apply your mind to it, so as to forget all your employments and recreations. It only requires of you, without putting these aside, to act towards God as you act on occasion towards those who love you and whom you love.

Your God is ever near you, no, within you: *In Him we live, and move, and be* (Acts 17:28). There is no barrier at the door against any who desire to speak with him; no, God delights that you should treat with him confidently. Treat with him of your business, your plans, your griefs, your fears — of all that concerns you. Above all, do so (as I have

8

said) with confidence, with open heart. For God is not inclined to speak to the soul that speaks not to him; since, if it is not used to converse with him, it would little understand his voice when he spoke to it. And this is what the Lord complains of: *Our sister is little: what shall we do to our sister in the day when she is to be spoken to?* (Cant. 8:8). Our sister is but a child in my love; what shall we do to speak to her if she understands me not? God will have himself esteemed the Lord of surpassing power and terribleness, when we despise his grace; but, on the contrary, he will have himself treated with as the most affectionate friend when we love him; and to this end he would have us often speak with him familiarly and without restraint.

It is true that God ought always to be revered in the highest degree; but when he favors you by making you feel his presence and know his desire that you should speak to him as to that one who loves you above all, then express to him your feelings with freedom and confidence. *She prevents them that covet her, so that she first shows herself unto them* (Wis. 6:14). When you desire his love, he takes the first step, without waiting till you come to him; and presents himself to you, bringing with him the graces and the remedies you stand in need of. He only waits for you to speak to him, to show you that he is near to you, ready to hear and to comfort you: *And His ears are unto their prayers* (Ps. 33:16).

By reason of his immensity, our God is in every place; but there are two places above all where he has his own peculiar dwelling. One is the highest heaven, where he is present by that glory which he communicates to the blessed; the other is upon earth—it is within the humble soul that loves him: *Who dwells with a contrite and humble spirit* (Isa. 57:15). He, then, our God, dwells in the height of heaven; and yet he disdains not to occupy and engage himself day and night with his faithful servants in their cabins or their cells. And there he bestows on them his divine consolations, each one of which surpasses all the delights the world can give, and which he only does not desire who has no experience of them: *Oh, taste and see that the Lord is sweet* (Ps. 33:9).

Friends in the world have some hours in which they converse together, and others during which they are apart; but between God and you, if you wish, there shall never be one hour of separation: *You shall rest, and your sleep shall be sweet: the Lord will be at your side* (Prov. 3:24). You may sleep, and God will place himself at your side, and watch with you continually: *I will repose myself with Him, and He shall be a comfort in my cares and grief* (Wis. 8:9-16). When you take your rest, he departs not from beside your pillow; he remains thinking

10

always of you, that when you wake in the night he may speak to you by his inspirations, and receive from you some act of love, of oblation, of thanksgiving; so as to keep up even in those hours his gracious and sweet converse with you. Sometimes also he will speak to you in your sleep, and cause you to hear his voice, that on waking you may put in practice what he has spoken: *I will speak to him in a dream* (Num. 12:6).

He is there also in the morning, to hear from you some word of affection, of confidence; to be the depositary of your first thoughts, and of all the actions which you promise to perform that day to please him; of all the griefs, too, which you offer to endure willingly for his glory and love. But as he fails not to present himself to you at the moment of your waking, fail not you, on your part, to give him immediately a look of love, and to rejoice when your God announces to you the glad tidings that he is not far from you, as once he was by reason of your sins; but that he loves you, and would be beloved by you: and at that same moment he gives you the gracious precept, *You shall love the Lord your God with your whole heart* (Deut. 6:5).

III

Of What, When, and How

1. IN GENERAL

NEVER, then, forget his sweet presence, as do the greater part of men. Speak to him as often as you can; for he does not grow weary of this nor disdain it, as do the lords of the earth. If you love him, you will not be at a loss what to say to him. Tell him all that occurs to you about yourself and your affairs, as you would tell it to a dear friend. Look not upon him as a haughty sovereign, who will only converse with the great, and on great matters. He, our God, delights to abase himself to converse with us, loves to have us communicate to him our smallest, our most daily concerns. He loves you as much, and has as much care for you, as if he had none others to think of but yourself. He is as entirely devoted to your interests as though the only end of his providence were to succor you, of his almighty power to aid you, of his mercy and goodness to take pity on you, to do you good, and gain by the delicate touches of his kindness your confidence and love. Manifest, then, to him freely all your state of mind, and pray to him to guide you to accomplish perfectly his

12

holy will. And let all your desires and plans be simply bent to discover his good pleasure, and do what is agreeable to his divine heart: *Commit your way to the Lord* (Ps. 36:5): *and desire of Him to direct your ways, and that all your counsels may abide in Him* (Tob. 4:20).

Say not, But where is the need of disclosing to God all my wants, if he already sees and knows them better than I? True, he knows them; but God makes as if he knew not the necessities about which you do not speak to him, and for which you seek not his aid. Our Savior knew well that Lazarus was dead, and yet he made as if he knew it not, until the Magdalene had told him of it, and then he comforted her by raising her brother to life again (John 11:1).

2. IN TRIALS

When, therefore, you are afflicted with any sickness, temptation, persecution, or other trouble, go at once and beseech him, that his hand may help you. It is enough for you to present the affliction before him; to come in and say, *Behold, O Lord, for I am in distress* (Lam. 1:20). He will not fail to comfort you, or at least to give you strength to suffer that grief with patience; and it will turn out a greater good to you than if he had altogether freed you from it. Tell him all the thoughts of fear or of sadness that torment you; and say to him, My God, in You are all my hopes; I offer to You this affliction, and resign myself to Your will; but do You take pity on me—either deliver me out of it, or give me strength to bear it. And he will truly keep with you that promise made in the Gospel to all those who are in trouble, to console and comfort them as often as they have recourse to him: *Come to Me, all you that labor and are burdened, and I will refresh you* (Matt. 11:28).

He will not be displeased that in your desolations you should go to your friends to find some relief; but he wills you chiefly to have recourse to himself. At all events, therefore, after you have applied to creatures, and they have been unable to comfort your heart, have recourse to your Creator, and say to him, Lord, men have only words for me; *my friends are full of words* (Job 16:21); they cannot comfort me, nor do I any more desire to be comforted by them; You are all my hope, all my love. From You only will I receive comfort; and let my comfort be, on this occasion, to do what pleases You. Behold me ready to endure this grief through my whole life, through all eternity, if such is Your good pleasure. Only do You help me.

Fear not that he will be offended if you sometimes gently complain, and say to him, *Why, O Lord, have You retired afar off?* (Ps. 9:22). You know, Lord, that I love You, and desire nothing but Your love; in pity help me, and forsake me not. And when the desolation lasts long, and troubles you exceedingly, unite your voice to that of Jesus in agony and dying on the cross, and beseech his mercy, saying, *My God, my God, why have You forsaken me?* (Matt. 27:46). But let the effect of this be to humble you yet more at the thought that he deserves no consolations who has offended God; and yet more to enliven your confidence, knowing that God does all things, and permits all, for your good: *All things work together unto good* (Rom. 8:28). Say with great courage, even when you feel most troubled and disconsolate: *The Lord is my light and my salvation; whom shall I fear?* (Ps. 26:1). Lord, it is Yours to enlighten me, it is Yours to save me; in You do I trust: *In You, O Lord, have I hoped; let me never be confounded* (Ps. 30:2). And thus keep yourself in peace, knowing there never was any one who placed his hopes in God and was lost: *No one has hoped in the Lord, and has been confounded* (Ecclus. 2:11). Consider, your God loves you more than you can love yourself; what do you fear? David comforted himself, saying, *The Lord is careful for me* (Ps. 39:18). Say to him, therefore, Lord, into Your arms I cast myself; I desire to have no thought but of loving and pleasing You; behold me ready to do what You require of me. You do not only will my good, You are careful for it; unto You, then, do I leave the care of my salvation. In You do I rest, and will rest for evermore, since You will that in You I should place all my hopes: *In peace, in the self-same, I will sleep and I will rest; for You, O Lord, singularly have settled me in hope* (Ps. 4:9).

Think of the Lord in goodness (Wis. 1:1). In these words the Wise Man exhorts us to have more confidence in the divine mercy than dread of the divine justice; since God is immeasurably more inclined to bestow favors than to punish; as St. James says, *Mercy exalts itself above judgment* (James 2:13). The Apostle St. Peter tells us that in all fears, whether about our interests for time or for eternity, we should commit ourselves altogether to the goodness of our God, who keeps the greatest care of our safety: *Casting all your care upon Him, for He has care of you* (1 Peter 5:7). Oh, what a beautiful meaning does this lend to the title which David gives to the Lord, when he says that our God is the God who makes it his care to save: *Our God is the God of salvation* (Ps. 67:21); which signifies, as Bellarmine explains it, that the office peculiar to the Lord is, not to condemn, but to save all. For while he threatens with his displeasure those who disregard him, he promises, on the other hand, his assured mercies to those who fear him; as the divine Mother said in her Canticle, *And His mercy is to them that fear*

16

Him. I set before you, devout soul, all these passages of Scripture, that when the thought disquiets you, Am I to be saved or not? Am I predestined or not? you may take courage, and understand from the promises he makes you what desire God has to save you, if only you are resolved to serve him and to love him as he demands at your hands.

3. IN JOYS

Further, when you receive pleasant news, do not act like those unfaithful, thankless souls who have recourse to God in time of trouble, but in time of prosperity forget and forsake him. Be as faithful to him as you would be to a friend who loves you and rejoices in your good; go at once and tell him of your gladness, and praise him and give him thanks, acknowledging it all as a gift from his hands; and rejoice in that happiness because it comes to you of his good pleasure. Rejoice, therefore, and comfort yourself in him alone: *I will rejoice in the Lord; and I will joy in God my Jesus* (Habac. 3:18). Say to him, My Jesus, I bless, and will ever bless You, for granting me so many favors, when I deserved at Your hands not favors, but chastisements for the affronts I have given You. Say to him, with the sacred Spouse, *All*

17

fruits, the new and the old, my Beloved, I have kept for You (Cant. 7:13). Lord, I give You thanks; I keep in memory all Your bounties, past and present, to render You praise and glory for them forever and ever.

But if you love your God, you ought to rejoice more in his blessedness than in your own. He who loves a friend very much sometimes takes more delight in that friend's good than if it had been his own. Comfort yourself, then, in the knowledge that your God is infinitely blessed. Often say to him, My beloved Lord, I rejoice more in Your blessedness than in any good of mine; yes, for I love You more than I love myself.

4. AFTER A FAULT

Another mark of confidence highly pleasing to your most loving God is this: that when you have committed any fault, you be not ashamed to go at once to his feet and seek his pardon. Consider that God is so greatly inclined to pardon sinners that he laments their perdition, when they depart far from him and live as dead to his grace. Therefore does he lovingly call them, saying, *Why will you die, O house of Israel? Return you, and live* (Ezek. 18:31). He promises to receive the soul that has forsaken him, so soon as she returns to his arms: *Turn you to me, . . . and I will turn to you* (Zach. 1:3). Oh, if sinners did but know with what tender mercy the Lord stands waiting to forgive them! *The Lord waits, that He may have mercy on you* (Isa. 30:18). Oh, did they but know the desire he has, not to chastise, but to see them converted, that he may embrace them, that he may press them to his heart! He declares: *As I live, says the Lord God, I desire not the death of the wicked, but that the wicked turn from his way and live* (Ezek. 33:11). He even says: *And then come and accuse Me, says the Lord: if your sins be as scarlet, they shall be made as white as snow* (Isa. 1:18). As though he had said, Sinners, repent of having offended Me, and then come unto Me: if I do not pardon you, "accuse Me"; upbraid Me, and treat Me as one unfaithful. But no, I will not be wanting to My promise. If you will come, know this: that though your consciences are dyed deep as crimson by your sins, I will make them by My grace as white as snow. In a word, he has declared that when a soul repents of having offended him, he forgets all its sins: *I will not remember all his iniquities* (Ezek. 18:22).

As soon, then, as you fall into any fault, raise your eyes to God, make an act of love, and with humble confession of your fault, hope assuredly for his pardon, and say to him, *Lord, behold he whom You love is sick* (John 11:3); that heart which You do love is sick, is full of sores: *heal my soul; for*

I have sinned against You (Ps. 40:5). You seek after penitent sinners; behold, here is one at Your feet, who has come in search of You. The evil is done already; what have I now to do? You will not have me lose courage: after this my sin You do still love me, and I too love You. Yes, my God, I love You with all my heart; I repent of the displeasure I have given You; I purpose never to do so any more. You, who are that God, *merciful and gracious, patient and of much compassion* (Ps. 85:5), forgive me; make me to hear what You did say to the Magdalene, *Your sins are forgiven you* (Luke 7:48); and give me strength to be faithful unto You for the time to come.

That you may not lose courage at such a moment, cast a glance at Jesus on the cross; offer his merits to the Eternal Father; and thus hope certainly for pardon, since he *spared not even His own Son* (Rom. 8:32). Say to him with confidence, *Look on the face of Your Christ* (Ps. 83:10). My God, behold Your Son, dead for my sake; and for the love of that Son forgive me. Attend greatly, devout soul, to the instruction commonly given by masters of the spiritual life, after your unfaithful conduct, at once to have recourse to God, though you have repeated it a hundred times in a day; and after your falls, and the recourse you have had to the Lord (as has been just said), at once to be in peace. Otherwise, while you remain cast down and disturbed at the fault you have committed, your converse with God will be small; your trust in him will fail; your desire to love him grow cold; and you will be little able to go forward in the way of the Lord. On the other hand, by having immediate recourse to God to ask his forgiveness, and to promise him amendment, your very faults will serve to advance you further in the divine love. Between friends who sincerely love each other it often happens that when one has displeased the other, and then humbles himself and asks pardon, their friendship thereby becomes stronger than ever. Do you likewise; see to it that your very faults serve to bind you yet closer in love to your God.

5. IN DOUBTS

In any kind of doubtfulness also, either on your own account or that of others, never leave acting towards your God with a confidence like to that of faithful friends, who consult together on every matter. So do you take counsel with himself, and beseech him to enlighten you that you may decide on what will be most pleasing to him: *Put those words in my mouth, and strengthen the resolution in my heart* (Judith 9:18). Lord, tell me what You would have me to do or to answer; and thus will I. *Speak, Lord; for Your servant hears* (1 Kings 3:10).

6. FOR YOUR NEIGHBOR

Use towards him also the freedom of recommending not only your own needs, but also those of others. How agreeable will it be to your God that sometimes you forget even your own interests to speak to him of the advancement of his glory, of the miseries of others, especially those who groan in affliction, of those souls, his spouses, who in purgatory sigh after the vision of himself, and of poor sinners who are living destitute of his grace! For these especially say to him: Lord, You who are so amiable, and worthy of an infinite love, how do You, then, endure to see such a number of souls in the world, on whom You have bestowed so many favors, and who yet will not know You, will not love You, no, even offend and despise You? Ah! my God, object of all love, make Yourself to be known, make Yourself to be beloved. "Hallowed be Thy name, Thy kingdom come"; may Your name be adored and beloved by all; may Your love reign in all hearts. Ah, let me not depart without granting me some grace for those unfaithful souls for whom I pray.

7. THE DESIRE FOR HEAVEN

It is said that in purgatory those souls who in this life have had but little longing for heaven are punished with a particular suffering, called the pain of languor; and with reason, because to long but little for heaven is to set small value on the great good of the eternal kingdom which our Redeemer has purchased for us by his death. Forget not, therefore, devout soul, frequently to sigh after heaven: say to your God that it seems to you an endless time for you to come and see him, and to love him face to face. Long ardently to depart out of this banishment, this scene of sinning, and danger of losing his grace, that you may arrive in that land of love where you may love him with all your powers. Say to him again and again, Lord, so long as I live on this earth, I am always in danger of forsaking You and losing Your love. When will it be that I quit this life, wherein I am ever offending You, and come to love You with all my soul, and unite myself to You, with no danger of losing You any more? St. Teresa was ever sighing in this way, and used to rejoice when she heard the clock strike, because another hour of life, and of the danger of losing God, was past and gone. For she so greatly desired death in order to see God, that she was dying with the desire to die; and hence she composed that loving canticle of hers, *I die, because I do not die.*

IV

God Answers the Soul That Speaks to Him

IN a word, if you desire to delight the loving heart of your God, be careful to speak to him as often as you are able, and with the fullest confidence that he will not disdain to answer and speak with you in return. He does not, indeed, make himself heard in any voice that reaches your ears, but in a voice that your heart can well perceive, when you withdraw from converse with creatures, to occupy yourself in conversing with your God alone: *I will lead her into the wilderness, and I will speak to her heart* (Osee 2:14). He will then speak to you by such inspirations, such interior lights, such manifestations of his goodness, such sweet touches in your heart, such tokens of forgiveness, such experience of peace, such hopes of heaven, such rejoicings within you, such sweetness of his grace, such loving and close embraces—in a word, such voices of love—as are well understood by those souls whom he loves, and who seek for nothing but himself alone.

V

Practical Summary

LASTLY, to make a brief summary of what has already been said at large, I will not omit to suggest a devout practice whereby you may fulfill all your daily actions in a manner pleasing to God.

When you wake in the morning, let it be your first thought to raise your mind to him, offering to his glory all that you shall do or suffer that day, praying to him to assist you by his grace. Then make your other morning acts of devotion, acts of thanksgiving and of love, prayers, and resolutions to live that day as though it were to be the last of your life. Father St. Jure recommends the making in the morning of a compact with the Lord; that every time you make a certain sign, as placing your hand upon your heart, or raising your eyes to heaven or to the crucifix, and the like, you wish thereby to make an act of love, of desire to see him loved by all, of oblation of yourself, and other acts of the same kind. When you have made these acts, and placed your soul in the side of Jesus and under the mantle of Mary, and have prayed the Eternal Father that for the love of Jesus and Mary he would protect you during the day, be careful, before you engage in anything else, to make your mental prayer, or meditation, at least for half an hour; and let your specially chosen meditation be the sorrow and the shame which Jesus Christ suffered in his Passion. This is the dearest subject to loving souls, and the one that most kindles divine love within them. If you would make spiritual progress, let three devotions be especially dear to you; devotion to the Passion of Jesus Christ, to the Most Holy Sacrament, and to the ever-blessed Virgin. In mental prayer, make again and again acts of contrition, of love to God, and oblation of yourself. The Venerable Father Charles Caraffa, founder of the Pious Workers, said that one fervent act of the love of God made thus in the morning is sufficient to maintain the soul in fervor throughout the whole day.

Then, besides the more specific acts of devotion, such as confession, Communion, recitation of the divine office, etc., whenever you are engaged in external occupations, as in study, in labor, or in any other employment that may be proper to your condition, never forget, when setting about it, to make an offering of it to God, praying for his assistance to enable you to perform it in a perfect manner; and do not omit to retire frequently into the cell of your heart, in order to unite yourself to God, according to the practice of St. Catherine of Sienna. In short, whatever you do, do it with and for God. In going out of your room or house, and on returning again, always commend yourself to the divine Mother, by saying a Hail Mary. When sitting down to meals, make an offering to God of the disgust or gratification you may find in what you eat and drink; and, on rising from table, return thanks to him and say, Lord, how great is Your goodness to one who has offended You so much! In the course of the day be careful to make your spiritual reading, to visit the Most Holy Sacrament and the Most Holy Mary; and in the evening to say the Rosary, and to make an examination of conscience, together with the Christian acts of faith, hope, charity, contrition, resolutions of amendment, and of receiving the Holy Sacraments during life and at the hour of death, forming also the intention of gaining all the indulgences that you can gain. And again, on going to bed, reflect that if you had your deserts, you would be lying down in the flames of hell; then, with the crucifix in your arms, compose yourself to sleep, saying, *In peace, in the self-same, I will sleep and take my rest* (Ps. 4:9).

That you may be able to keep yourself ever in a state of recollection and union with God, as long as you live, and as far as may be possible, turn everything that you may see or hear into an occasion for raising your mind to God, or for taking a glance at eternity. For example, when you see running water, reflect that your life is also in like manner running on, and carrying you nearer and nearer to death. When you see a lamp going out for want of oil, reflect that thus also one day you will have to bring your life to its end. When you see the graves or remains of the dead, consider that you also have to become like them. When you see the great ones of this world rejoicing in their wealth or distinction, pity their folly, and say, For me God is sufficient: *Some trust in chariots, some in horses, but we in the name of the Lord* (Ps. 19:8). Let these glory in such vanity; I will make nothing my glory but the grace of God, and the love of him. When you behold the pompous funerals, or the fine sepulchral monuments of the great ones who are dead, say, If these are damned, what is the good of this pomp to them? When you behold the sea in a calm or a storm, consider the difference that there is between a soul when in the grace and when out of the grace of God. When you see a tree that is withered, consider that a soul without God is serviceable for nothing but to be cast into fire. If you ever happen to see one who has been guilty of some great crime, trembling with shame and fright in the presence of his judge, or of his father, or of his bishop, consider what the panic of a sinner will be in the presence of Christ his judge. When it thunders, and you become alarmed, reflect how those miserable ones who are damned tremble as they hear continually in hell the thunders of the divine wrath. If you ever see one who has been condemned to suffer a painful death, and who says, Is there, then, no longer any means for my escaping death? consider what will be the despair of a soul when it is condemned to hell, as it says, Is there, then, no longer any means for escaping from eternal ruin?

When your eye rests on scenes in the country or along the shore, on flowers or fruits, and you are delighted by the sight and scent of all, say, Behold, how many are the beautiful creatures that God has created for me in this world, in order that I may love him; and what further enjoyments does he not keep prepared for me in Paradise? St. Teresa used to say that when she saw any beautiful hills or slopes, they seemed to reproach her for her own ingratitude to God. And the Abbot de Rancé, founder of La Trappe, said that the beautiful creatures around him reminded him of his own obligation to love God. St. Augustine also said the same, crying out aloud, "Heaven, and earth, and all things tell me to love You" (*Conf.* l. 10, c. 6). It is related of a certain holy man, that in passing through the fields he would strike with a little stick the flowers and plants which he found, saying, "Be silent; do not reproach me any longer for my ingratitude to God. I have understood you; be silent; say no more." When St. Mary Magdalene of Pazzi held in her hand any beautiful fruit or flower, she used to feel herself smitten by it with divine love, saying to herself, "Behold, my God has thought from eternity of creating this fruit, this flower, in order to give it me as a token of the love which he bears towards me."

When you see rivers or brooks, reflect that as the water which you behold keeps running on to the ocean without ever stopping, so ought you to be ever hasting on to God, who is your only good. When you happen to be in a vehicle that is drawn by beasts of burden, say, See what labor these innocent animals go through for my service; and how much pains do I myself take in order to serve and please my God? When you see a little dog, which for a miserable morsel of bread is so faithful to its master, reflect how much greater reason you have to be faithful to God, who has created and preserved and provided for you, and heaps upon you so many blessings. When you hear the birds sing, say, Listen, O my soul, to the praise which these little creatures are giving to their Creator; and what are you doing? Then do you also praise him with acts of love. On the other hand, when you hear the cock crow, recall to your memory that there once was a time when you also, like Peter, denied your God; and renew your contrition and your tears. So, likewise, when you see the house or place where you have sinned, turn yourself to God, and say, *The sins of my youth and my ignorance remember not, O Lord* (Ps. 24:7).

When you behold any valleys, consider that as their fertility is owing to the waters that run down from the mountains, so from heaven do graces descend upon the souls of the humble, and pass by the proud. When you see a beautifully ornamented church, consider the beauty of a soul in a state of grace, which is a real temple of God. When you behold the sea, consider the immensity and the greatness of God. When you see fire, or candles lighted on an altar, say, How many years is it since I ought to have been cast into hell to burn? But since You, O Lord, have not sent me there, make this heart of mine burn with love for You, as that wood or those candles burn. When you look up at the sky, all studded with stars, say with St. Andrew of Avellino, "O my feet, you will one day have those stars beneath you."

Then, in order frequently to recall to mind the mysteries of our Savior's love, when you see hay, a manger, or caves, let the Infant Jesus in the stable of Bethlehem be present to your recollection. When you see a saw, a hammer, a plane, or an axe, remember how Jesus worked like a mere lad, in the shop at Nazareth. Then if you see ropes, thorns, nails, or pieces of wood, reflect on the Passion and Death of our Redeemer. St. Francis of Assisi, on seeing a lamb, would begin to weep, saying, "My Lord like a lamb was led to death for me." Again: when you see altars, chalices, or patens, recall to mind the greatness of the love which Jesus Christ has borne us in giving us the Most Holy Sacrament of the Eucharist.

Frequently during the day make an offering of yourself to God, as St. Teresa used to do, saying, "Lord, here am I; do with me that which pleases You. Declare to me Your will, that I may do it for You; I wish to do it thoroughly." Then repeat, as often as you can, acts of love towards God. St. Teresa used also to say that acts of love are the fuel by which holy love is to be kept on fire within the heart. When the Venerable Sister Seraphine of Carpi was one day considering that the mule belonging to the convent had not the power of loving God, she expressed her compassion for it thus: "Poor brute; you neither know nor can love your God"; and the mule commenced to weep so that the tears fell in streams from its eyes: so likewise do you, when beholding any animal which has not the capacity for knowing or loving God, animate yourself, who can love him, to make the more abundant acts of love. Whenever you fall into any fault, humble yourself for it immediately; and, with an act of more fervent love, endeavor to rise again. When anything adverse happens, immediately make an offering to God of what you have to suffer, bringing your will into conformity with his own; and ever accustom yourself under all adverse circumstances to repeat these words: "Thus God wills; thus I will too." Acts of resignation are the acts of love that are most precious and acceptable to the heart of God.

When you have to decide upon anything, or to give any counsel of importance, first commend yourself to God, and then set about your undertaking, or give your opinion. As often as you can during the day, after the example of St. Rose of Lima, repeat the prayer, *Deus in adjutorium meum intende:* "Lord, come to my assistance; do not leave me in my own hands." And for this end frequently turn to the image of the Crucified, or to that of the Most Holy Mary, which is in your room; and do not omit to make frequent invocations of the names of Jesus and of Mary, especially in time of temptation. Since God is infinite goodness, his desire of communicating his graces to us is perfect. The Venerable Father Alvarez one day saw our Savior with his hands full of graces, and going about in search of those to whom he might dispense them. But it is his will that we should ask them of him. *Ask, and you shall receive* (John 16:24), otherwise he will draw back his hand; whereas, on the contrary, he will willingly open it to those who call upon him. And who is there, says the Preacher, that has called upon him and God despised him by not granting his prayer? *Who has called upon Him, and He has despised him?* (Ecclus. 2:12). And David tells us that the Lord shows not merely mercy, but great mercy, to those who call upon him: *For You, O Lord, are sweet and mild and plentiful in mercy to all that call upon You* (Ps. 85:5).

Oh, how good and bountiful is the Lord to him who seeks him lovingly! *The Lord is good to the soul that seeks Him* (Lam. 3:25). If he lets himself be found even by him who seeks him not—*I was found by them that did not seek Me* (Rom. 10:20) —how much more willingly will he let himself be found by one who seeks him—and seeks him, too, in order to serve him and to love him!

To conclude: St. Teresa says that holy souls in this world have to conform themselves by love to what the souls of the blessed do in heaven. As the saints in heaven occupy themselves only with God, and have no other thought or joy than in his glory and in his love, so also must this be the case with you. While you are in this world, let God be your only happiness, the only object of your affections, the only end of all your actions and desires, until you come to that eternal kingdom where your love will be in all things perfected and completed, and your desires will be perfectly fulfilled and satisfied.

A SHORT TREATISE ON PRAYER

A SHORT TREATISE ON PRAYER

I

The Necessity of Prayer

IT is blasphemy to say with Luther and Calvin that the fall of Adam has made it impossible for men to keep God's law; and it is also an error, condemned by the Church, to say with Jansenius that some precepts are impossible even to the just, with their present strength, and that God does not give them aid to enable them to fulfill them. Now the Council of Trent has declared that God does not command impossibilities, but admonishes us to do what we can with the assistance of the ordinary grace with which we are always furnished, and then pray to him to give us the further grace requisite to enable us to fulfill that which otherwise is beyond our strength, upon which he gives us the assistance which we require. In the words of the Council, "God does not command impossible things; but, by commanding, he admonishes you both to do what you can, and to pray for that which is beyond your strength;

37

and he assists you, so as to make you able to do it"
(*Sess.* 6, c. 11). Hence many sound theologians*
teach that God gives, or at least offers, to all men
either the grace which immediately enables them
actually to fulfill the commandments, or at any
rate the remote grace which enables them to pray,
and by means of prayer to obtain the proximate
grace by which they can actually observe the
commandments of God.

Yet, for all this, there can be no doubt that the
observance of the law, in the present state of our
corrupt nature, is very difficult, and even morally
impossible without a special assistance of God,
and more abundant than that which man required
in the state of innocence. Now, ordinarily
speaking, says the celebrated Gennade (*De Eccl.
Dogm.* c. 26), God only gives this special assistance
to those who pray for it. St. Augustine teaches,
that with the exception of the first motions o f
grace — such as the first call to faith or to penance,
which come to us without our concurrence — all
other graces, and especially that of perseverance,

*See Habert (*Theol. Græc. Pat.* l. 2, c. 6, n. 1; c. 15, n. 2 and
3); the latter quotes Gamache, Duval, Isambert, Le Moyne,
etc., and asserts that such is the common opinion of the
schools, notably that of the Sorbonne. See also Thomassin
(*Theol. dogm. tr. de Grat.* c. 8), Duplessis d'Argentré (*Diss. de
mult. gen. div. gr.*), Tournely (*Præl. Theol. de gr. chr.* q. 7, a. 4,
concl. 5).

are only given to those persons who pray for them: "We believe that no one comes to be saved, except by the call of God. That no one works out his own salvation, except by the assistance of God; and that no one merits this assistance, except by prayer" (*De Dono pers.* c. 16). And elsewhere he assumes it as certain, "that God gives us a few things even when we do not pray, such as the beginnings of faith; but that he has provided the rest only for those who pray."

From this theologians, such as Suarez, Habert, Layman, F. Segneri, and others, with Clement of Alexandria, St. Basil, St. Augustine, and St. Chrysostom, conclude that prayer is necessary to adults, if not as an end, yet as a means; that is to say, in the ordinary course of Providence, no Christian can be saved without recommending himself to God, and asking him for the graces necessary for his salvation. St. Chrysostom says that as the soul is necessary for the life of the body, so is prayer necessary for the soul to preserve it in the grace of God (*De or. D.* l. 1). This, too, is the meaning of those words of Jesus Christ: *Men ought always to pray, and not to faint* (Luke 18:1). Men ought—it is necessary for them always to pray. St. James teaches us the same thing: *You have not because you ask not* (James 4:2); and the same lesson is taught us in that short sentence which our Savior spoke: *Ask, and it shall be given you*

(John 16:24). If, then, says St. Teresa, he who asks
obtains, he that does not ask does not obtain. God
wishes the salvation of all men: *He wills all men to
be saved* (1 Tim. 2:4); but he wills that we should
ask him for the graces which are necessary for our
salvation. Shall we refuse to do such a little thing
as this?

Let us conclude this first point by gathering
from what we have said, that he who prays is
certain to be saved; while he who prays not is
certain to be damned. All the saints were saved,
and came to be saints by praying; all the accursed
souls in hell were lost through neglect of prayer; if
they had prayed, it is certain that they would not
have been lost. And this will be one of the greatest
occasions of their anguish in hell, the thought that
they might have saved themselves so easily; that
they had only to beg God to help them, but that
now the time is past when this could avail them.

II

The Efficacy of Prayer

THE Holy Scriptures are full of texts in which God tells us that he hears all our prayers. In one place he says: *He shall cry to Me, and I will hear him* (Ps. 90:15). In another, *Cry to me and I will hear you* (Jer. 33:3). Again: *Call upon Me in the day of trouble, and I will deliver you* (Ps. 49:15). You shall cry, and I will deliver you from the danger of being damned. Again: *Who has called upon Him, and He despised Him?* (Ecclus. 2:12). Has it ever occurred that God has turned a deaf ear to the prayers of any one that called upon him? Again: *At the voice of your cry, as soon as He shall hear, He will answer you* (Isa. 30:19). He will hear and respond to your prayer immediately. Again: *As they are yet speaking, I will hear* (Isa. 65:24). Before they have time to finish their petitions, I will answer them. Again: *Blessed be God, who has not turned away my prayer nor His mercy from me* (Ps. 65:20). Our prayer is always accompanied by God's mercy; hence, St. Augustine remarks upon this text, that when we find ourselves calling on God we ought to feel very happy, because when we are praying we ought to feel certain that God is hearing us: "When you see that your prayer is not removed from you, be sure that his mercy is not removed

41

from you either" (*Enarr. in Ps.* 65). Again: *You shall ask whatever you will, and it shall be done to you* (John 15:7). Ask what you like; it is enough to ask, and it shall be granted to you.

Hence Theodoret says that prayer is omnipotent: "It is one, but can obtain all things" (*Oratio, cum sit una, omnia potest*). And St. Bonaventure says that by prayer we obtain every good, and are delivered from every evil: "By it is obtained the enjoyment of every good, and deliverance of every ill" (in *Luc.* c. 11). And if, adds St. Bernard, at times God does not give us the grace which we ask, we ought to feel quite convinced that he is giving us in its stead some grace that is more needful to us. O Lord, said David, You are full of pity and mercy to all those who pray to You: *You, O Lord, are sweet, and mild, and plentiful in mercy to all that call upon You* (Ps. 85:5). And St. James says, *If any of you want wisdom, let him ask of God, who gives to all abundantly, and upbraids not* (James 1:5). To those who pray, God gives with no sparing hand, as do the rich of this world, for their wealth soon comes to an end; but God's riches are infinite, and the more he gives the more he has to give, and therefore he gives abundantly, with unsparing hand, far surpassing anything that we can ask. *And upbraids not;* does not cast in our teeth the insults we have offered him when we go to ask favors of him.

The Efficacy of Prayer

The nature of goodness is to be diffusive; and therefore God, whose very essence is infinite goodness ("his nature is goodness"—*Deus cujus natura bonitas*—says St. Leo), has the greatest possible desire to communicate to us his good things and his own happiness, and is therefore anxious for our good. *The Lord is careful for me* (Ps. 39:18), said David; and this made the royal prophet exclaim, *In whatsoever day I shall call upon You, behold I know that You are my God* (Ps. 55:10). O Lord, he would say, whenever I call upon You, I at once know that You are my God; that is, that You are the infinite goodness, who desire us to pray to You, to give You an opportunity to shower Your benefits upon us; for as soon as we begin to ask You for grace, You do at once give it. One day a miserable leper presented himself to our Savior, and said to him, *Lord, if You will, You can make me clean*; and Jesus answered, *I will; be you made clean* (Matt. 8:3), as though he had said, Ah, my child, do you doubt of my willingness to cure you? Do you not know that I am your God, and that my desire is to see all my creatures happy? And for what cause am I come down from heaven to earth, if not to make all men happy? Yes, I will; be you healed.

Many persons complain that God does not give them the graces which they wish for. But, says St. Bernard, how much reason has God to

43

complain of them that they do not pray, and that by this neglect they close his hand, which he would be so glad to open for their benefit? "Many complain that grace fails them; but much more justly might grace complain that many fail her" (*De Div.* s. 17). No, do not complain of me, says our Lord, if you have not received from me the graces of which you stood in need; complain of yourselves for not having asked me for them, which is the real reason why you have not received them; pray for them from this day forward, and you shall be satisfied to the full: *Until now you have not asked anything. Ask, and you shall receive, that your joy may be full* (John 16:24).

The monks of old once held a council among themselves to examine which was the most useful exercise to secure eternal salvation, and they concluded that it was to beseech God in prayer, with the words, *Incline unto my aid, O God!* (Ps. 69:2). And F. Paul Segneri tells us that when he began the practice of meditation, his chief object was to elicit affections; but that afterwards, when he came to know the great utility and necessity of prayer, he was careful to make it the principal part of his meditation.

III

The Conditions Required for Prayer

BUT how does it come to pass that some persons pray, but yet do not receive? They pray, indeed, but they do not pray as they ought, and this is why they obtain nothing: *You ask and receive not, because you ask wrongly* (James 4:3). Many persons seek for grace, but do not observe the proper conditions. Let us see, then, what are the necessary conditions of prayer, in order to make it efficacious to obtain the graces we desire.

1. HUMILITY

Prayer must be humble: *God resists the proud, but gives grace to the humble* (James 4:6). Here St. James tells us that God does not listen to the prayers of the proud, but resists them; while, on the other hand, he is always ready to hear the prayers of the humble: *The prayer of the man that humbles himself shall pierce the clouds, . . . and he will not depart till the Most High behold* (Ecclus. 35:21). The prayer of a humble soul at once penetrates the heavens and presents itself before the throne of God, and will not depart from there till God regards it and listens to it. However sinful such a soul may be,

God can never despise a heart that repents of its sins, and humbles itself: *A contrite and humbled heart, O God, You will not despise* (Ps. 50:19).

2. CONFIDENCE

Prayer must be confident: *No one has hoped in the Lord and been disappointed* (Ecclus. 2:11). The Holy Ghost assures us that it never has happened that any one who placed his trust in God has been deceived. He once said to St. Gertrude that a person who prays to him with confidence does him, in a certain way, such violence that he cannot but listen to him and grant all his requests. "Prayer," said St. John Climacus, "is a pious way of forcing God" (*Scal. par.* gr. 28). Prayer does violence to him; but a violence which he loves and delights in. "This violence is pleasing to God" (*Apolog.*). In the "Our Father," which is the prayer which Jesus Christ himself taught us as a means whereby to obtain all the graces necessary for our salvation, how are we made to address God? Not as Lord, not as Judge, but as Father, "our Father," because he wishes us to ask God for grace with the same confidence as a son, when he is hungry or ill, asks his own father for food or medicine. If a son is famished, he has only to tell his father, and he will be immediately fed; if he has been bitten by a venomous serpent, he has only to show the wound, and his father will apply the best remedy that he has. For this cause, our Savior has told us: *All things whatsoever you ask when you pray, believe that you shall receive, and they shall come unto you* (Mark 11:24). We have, then, only to pray to God with confidence in order to obtain all that we desire. And how could our Lord have exhorted us so earnestly to pray for grace, unless he had wished to give it? "He would not have exhorted us (says St. Augustine) to ask, unless he had been willing to grant" (*Serm.* 105 E. B.). The woman of Canaan whose daughter was possessed by a devil went to beseech Jesus Christ to deliver her from him, and said, "Have mercy on me, my daughter is grievously vexed by a devil." Jesus answered, *I am not sent except to the sheep of Israel* (Matt. 15:24); my mission is not to you Gentiles, only to the Jews. Yet she did not lose heart, but confidently repeated her prayer: O Lord, You can console me: *Lord help me!* (Matt. 15:25). Jesus replied, But the children's bread must not be given to dogs: *It is not good to take the bread of the children, and to give it to dogs* (Matt. 15:26). But, Lord, she replied, even the dogs are allowed the crumbs of bread which fall from the table: "Even the whelps eat of the crumbs." Upon which our Lord, having proved the great confidence of the woman, praised her for it, and did what she asked: *O woman, great is your faith; be it done to you as you will; and her daughter was healed from that hour* (Matt. 15:28).

Thus, confidence is necessary to obtain what we ask of God. But on what, it may be said, are we to found this confidence? On what? on the goodness of God, and on the promise which he made when he said, *Ask, and you shall receive* (John 16:24). "Who," says St. Augustine, "fears to be deceived when the Truth promises?" (*Conf.* l. 12, c. 1). Who can ever fear that what is promised will not be given to him, when it is God, the sovereign truth, who has promised?

3. PERSEVERANCE

Prayer should be persevering, otherwise it will not obtain eternal life. The grace of salvation is not a single grace, but is a chain of graces all united with the grace of final perseverance. Now to this chain of graces there must be a corresponding chain of prayers on our part. There is in St. Luke (chap. 11) a parable of a man who, to rid himself of the importunity of his friend, got out of bed, and gave him the loaves which he wanted. On this St. Augustine says: "Now, if this man, simply to rid himself of the importunity of his friend, would, against his will, give him the bread which he asked for, how much more will the good God give, who exhorts us to ask him?" (*Serm.* 61 E. B.). How much more will God, who has such a desire to make us partakers of his good things, dispense to us his graces when we ask him for them! Especially as he commands us to beg of him, and is displeased when we do not do so. God then wishes to grant us eternal life, and all the graces necessary for its attainment; but he also wishes us to be persevering in prayer. As Cornelius à Lapide says on this parable, "h e wishes us to be persevering in prayer, so as to be even importunate" (in *Luc.* xi. 8). Men cannot endure importunity; but God not only endures it, but wishes us to be importunate in begging for his grace, and especially for the grace of final perseverance.

It is true that we cannot merit final per-severance, as the Council of Trent has declared (*Sess.* 6, c. 13); for it is a gift that God gives us quite gratuitously; nevertheless St. Augustine tells us that perseverance may, in a certain way, be merited by prayer: "This gift of God may be merited in the way of begging; that is, it may be obtained by supplication" (*De Dono pers.* c. 6). So that the man who asks for perseverance, though he cannot merit it, will yet, as Suarez says, infallibly obtain it. But, says Bellarmine, "it is not enough to ask for it once, we must ask it daily, in order to obtain it daily" (*Quotidie petenda est, u t quotidie obtineatur*). And therefore Jesus Christ says, *Men ought always pray, and not to faint* (Luke 18:1). We must never cease from prayer; for when we do so, temptation may overcome us: *Watch you therefore, praying at all times, that you may be accounted worthy to escape all these things that are to come, and to stand before the Son of Man* (Luke 21:36). "Be watchful in continual prayer," says Jesus Christ, "that I may not have to drive you from Me when you stand before My judgment-seat." Well, therefore, does St. Paul admonish his disciples: *Pray without ceasing* (1 Thess. 5:17). Pray, and never cease to pray.

Blessed is the man that hears Me, and that watches daily at My doors (Prov. 8:34). God pronounces him to be blessed who continually watches at the doors of his mercy. And therefore, in the following words of the Gospel, Jesus Christ not only exhorts us, but also commands us, to pray (for prayer is not only a counsel, but a precept): *Ask, and it shall be given you; seek, and you shall find; knock, and it shall be opened to you* (Luke 11:9). It might seem enough to have said "ask," without adding "seek" and "knock." But no, this repetition is not superfluous; for this was our Savior's way of teaching us to do like the poor beggars, who, if they do not at once receive the relief they demand and are turned away, still keep on demanding it over and over again, and then begin knocking at the door, and insist on seeing the master of the house, and, indeed, make themselves exceedingly importunate and troublesome. This is how our Lord wishes us to do; to pray, and pray again, and never cease praying him to assist us, to keep his hand over us, and never to permit us to separate ourselves from him by sin. And this we should do, not only when we rise in the morning, but oftentimes during the day: when we hear Mass, when we make our meditation, when we make our thanksgiving after Communion, when we pay our visit to the Blessed Sacrament, when we examine our conscience at night, but, above all, when we are assailed by any temptation, especially if it is a temptation to impurity; the man who does not in this case have recourse to God, and at least invoke the holy names of Jesus and Mary, will scarcely be able to avoid falling.

IV

God Hears the Prayers of Sinners

BUT a person might say, I am a sinner, and God does not hear sinners, as we read in St. John's Gospel: *God does not hear sinners* (John 9:31). I answer, that these words were not spoken by our Lord, but by the man who had been born blind. And the proposition, if taken absolutely, is false; there is only one case in which it is true, as St. Thomas says, and that is when sinners pray as sinners (*Summa Theol*. 2. 2. q. 83, a. 16, ad 2); that is, ask something that they require to assist them in their sin; as, for instance, if a man asked God to help him to take vengeance of his enemy; in such cases God certainly will not hear. But when a man prays and asks for those things that are requisite for his salvation, what matters it whether he is a sinner or not? Suppose he were the greatest criminal in the world, let him only pray, he will surely obtain all that he asks.

The promise is general for all men; every one that seeks obtains: *Every one that asks receives* (Luke 11:10). "It is not necessary," says St. Thomas, "that the man who prays should merit the grace for which he asks." "By prayer we obtain even those things which we do not deserve" (*Summa Theol*. 1. 2. q. 114, a. 9, ad 1). In order to receive, it is enough to pray. The reason is (in the words of the same holy Doctor), "merit is grounded on justice, but the power of prayer (*impetratio*) is grounded on grace" (*Summa Theol.* 2. 2. q. 83, a. 16, ad 2). The power of prayer to obtain what we ask does not depend on the merit of the person who prays, but on the mercy and faithfulness of God, who has gratuitously, and of his own mere goodness, promised to hear the man who prays to him. When we pray, it is not necessary that we should be friends of God in order to obtain grace; indeed, the act of prayer, as St. Thomas says, makes us his friends: "Prayer itself makes us of the family of God" (*Comp. Theol.* p. 2, c. 2). And that which we cannot obtain through friendship, we may (as St. Chrysostom in a similar way affirms) obtain by prayer: "That which friendship could not accomplish, has been accomplished by prayer" (*Hom. Non esse desp.*). And Jesus Christ, to give us more encouragement to pray, and to assure us of obtaining grace when we pray, has made us that great and special promise: *Amen, amen, I say to you, if you ask the Father anything in My name, He will give it you* (John 16:23). As though he had said, Come, sinners, you have no merits of your own for which My Father should listen to you. But this is what you must do; when you want grace, ask for it in My name, and through My merits, and I promise you ("Amen, amen, I say to you," amounts to a kind of oath) you may depend on it, that whatever you ask, you shall obtain from My Father: *Whatever you shall ask, He will give it you.* Oh, what a sweet consolation for a poor sinner, to know that his sins are no hindrance to his obtaining every grace he asks for, since Jesus Christ has promised that whatever we ask of God, through his merits, he will grant it all!

V

God Has Pledged to Grant Us Spiritual Goods

IT is, however, necessary to understand that our Lord's promise to hear our prayers does not apply to our petitions for temporal goods, but only to those for spiritual graces necessary, or at any rate useful, for the salvation of the soul; so that we can only expect to obtain the graces which we ask in the name and through the merits of Jesus Christ, as we said just now. "But," as St. Augustine says, "if we ask anything prejudicial to our salvation, it cannot be said to be asked in the name of the Savior" (in *Joan.* tr. 102). That which is injurious to salvation cannot be expected from the Savior; God does not and cannot grant it; and why? because he loves us. A physician who has any regard for a sick man will not permit him to have food which he knows will injure him. And how many people would be prevented from committing the sins which they do commit if they were poor or sick? Many people ask for health or riches, but God does not give them, because he sees they would be an occasion of sin, or at least of growing lukewarm in his service. So when we ask these temporal gifts, we ought always to add this condition, if they are profitable for our souls. And when we see that God does not give them, let us rest assured that he refuses them only because he loves us, and because he sees that the things which we ask would only damage our spiritual well-being.

And often we ask God to deliver us from some troublesome temptation, which would persuade us to forfeit his grace; but God does not deliver us, in order that our soul may be more closely united in love with him. It is not temptations or bad thoughts that hurt us, and separate us from God, but consent to evil. When the soul, through the assistance of God's grace, resists a temptation, it makes a great advance in the way of perfection. St. Paul tells us that he was very much troubled with temptations to impurity, and that he prayed God three times to deliver him from them: *A sting of my flesh, an angel of Satan, was given me to buffet me; for which thing I besought the Lord thrice that it might depart from me* (2 Cor. 12:7-8). And what did the Lord answer? He told him, It is enough for you to have my grace: *My grace is sufficient for you* (2 Cor. 12:9). Thus should we, in the temptations which assault us, pray God to deliver us from them, or at least to help us to resist them. And when we thus pray, we should be quite certain that God is already helping us to resist them: *You did call upon Me in affliction, and I delivered you. I heard you in the secret place of tempest* (Ps. 80:8). Often does God leave us in the storm for our greater good; but still he hears us in secret, and gives us his grace to strengthen us to resist and to be resigned.

So, I repeat, all temporal gifts which are not necessary for salvation ought to be asked conditionally; and if we see that God does not give them, we must feel sure that he refuses them for our greater good. But with regard to spiritual graces, we must be certain that God gives them to us when we ask him. St. Teresa says that God loves us more than we love ourselves. And St. Augustine has declared that God has a greater desire to give us his grace than we have to receive it: "He is more willing to bestow his favors upon you, than you are desirous of receiving them" (*Serm.* 105 E. B.). And after him, St. Mary Magdalene of Pazzi has said that God feels a kind of obligation to the soul that prays, and, as it were, says to it, "Soul, I thank you that you ask me for grace." For then the soul gives him an opportunity of doing good to it, and of thus satisfying his desire of giving his grace to all. And how can it ever happen that God will not hear a soul that asks for the things which he most delights to give? When the soul says, "Lord, I ask You not for riches, honors, the goods of this world, but I only beg for Your grace; deliver me from sin, give me a good death, give me Paradise, and meanwhile give me Your love" (which is the grace that, as St. Francis de Sales says, we ought to pray for above all others), "give me resignation to Your will" (which is the virtue in which the whole of the love of God consists) — when the soul prays thus, how is it possible that God should refuse to hear it? And what prayers, O my God, will You ever hear (says St. Augustine), if You hear not those which are made as You wish them to be made: "If You hear not these, what do you hear?" (*De Civ. D.* l. 22, c. 8). And St. Bernard says, that when we ask for spiritual graces of this kind, the desire of obtaining them can only come to us from God himself; so the saint turns to God, and says to him, "Why have You given the desire, unless You were willing to satisfy it?" (*Desiderium ad quid dares, nisi velles exaudire?*). Since You, O Lord, do put into my heart to ask for these graces, I ought to be certain that You are willing to hear my prayer. But above all, the words of Jesus Christ ought to revive our confidence, when we are praying for spiritual graces: *If you, then, being evil, know how to give good gifts to your children, how much more will your Father from heaven give the Good Spirit to them that ask him?* (Luke 11:13). If you, who are full of evil, and of self-love, are unable to refuse your children the good things which they ask, how much more will your heavenly Father, who loves you more than any earthly father can love his family, grant you his spiritual gifts, when you ask him for them?

VI

Conclusion

LET us pray, then, and let us always be asking for grace, if we wish to be saved. Let prayer be our most delightful occupation; let prayer be the exercise of our whole life. And when we are asking for particular graces, let us always pray for the grace to continue to pray for the future; because if we leave off praying we shall be lost. There is nothing easier than prayer. What does it cost us to say, Lord, stand by me! Lord, help me! give me Your love! and the like? What can be easier than this? But if we do not do so, we cannot be saved. Let us pray, then, and let us always shelter ourselves behind the intercession of Mary: "Let us seek for grace, and let us seek it through Mary" (in *Serm. De Aquæd.*), says St. Bernard. And when we recommend ourselves to Mary, let us be sure that she hears us and obtains for us whatever we want. She cannot lack either the power or the will to help us, as the same saint says: "Neither means nor will can be wanting to her" (*De Assumpt.* s. 1). And St. Augustine addresses her: "Remember, O most pious Lady, that it has never been heard that any one who fled to your protection was forsaken" (in *Cant. post Psalt.*). Remember that the case has never occurred of a person having recourse to you, and having been abandoned. Ah, no, says St. Bonaventure, he who invokes Mary, finds salvation; and therefore he calls her "the salvation of those who invoke her." Let us, then, in our prayers always invoke Jesus and Mary; and let us never neglect to pray.

I have done. But before concluding, I cannot help saying how grieved I feel when I see that though the Holy Scriptures and the Fathers so often recommend the practice of prayer, yet so few other religious writers, or confessors, or preachers, ever speak of it; or if they do speak of it, just touch upon it in a cursory way, and leave it. But I, seeing the necessity of prayer, say, that the great lesson which all spiritual books should inculcate on their readers, all preachers on their hearers, and all confessors on their penitents, is this, to pray always; thus they should admonish them to pray; pray, and never give up praying. If you pray, you will be certainly saved; if you do not pray, you will be certainly damned.

PRAYER

Eternal Father, I humbly adore You, and thank You for having created me, and for having redeemed me through Jesus Christ. I thank You most sincerely for having made me a Christian, by giving me the true faith, and by adopting me as Your son, in the sacrament of baptism. I thank You for having, after the numberless sins I had committed, waited for my repentance, and for having pardoned (as I humbly hope) all the offences which I have offered to You, and for which I am now sincerely sorry, because they have been displeasing to You, who are infinite goodness. I thank You for having preserved me from so many relapses, of which I would have been guilty if You had not protected me. But my enemies still continue, and will continue till death, to combat against me, and to endeavor to make me their slave. If You do not constantly guard and succor me with your aid, I, a miserable creature, shall return to sin, and shall certainly lose Your grace. I beseech You, then, for the love of Jesus Christ, to grant me holy perseverance unto death. Jesus, Your Son, has promised that You will grant whatsoever we ask in his name. Through the merits, then, of Jesus Christ, I beg, for myself and for all the just, the grace never again to be separated from Your love, but to love You forever, in time and eternity. Mary, Mother of God, pray to Jesus for me.

MENTAL PRAYER

MENTAL PRAYER

I

Morally Necessary for Salvation

1. IT ENLIGHTENS THE MIND

IN the first place, without mental prayer the soul is without light. They, says St. Augustine, who keep their eyes shut cannot see the way to their country. The eternal truths are all spiritual things that are seen, not with the eyes of the body, but with the eyes of the mind; that is, by reflection and consideration. Now, they who do not make mental prayer do not see these truths, neither do they see the importance of eternal salvation, and the means which they must adopt in order to obtain it. The loss of so many souls arises from the neglect of considering the great affair of our salvation, and what we must do in order to be saved. *With desolation*, says the prophet Jeremias, *is all the land made desolate: because there is none that considers in the heart* (Jer. 12:11). On the other hand, the Lord says that he who keeps before his eyes the truths of faith—that is, death, judgment, and the happy or unhappy eternity that awaits us—shall never fall into sin. *In all your works remember your last end, and you shall never sin* (Ecclus. 7:40). Draw near to God, says David, and you shall be enlightened. *Come you to Him and be enlightened* (Ps. 33:6). In another place, our Savior says, *Let your loins be girt, and lamps burning in your hands* (Luke 12:35). These lamps are, according to St. Bonaventure, holy meditations (*Oratio est lucerna*); for in prayer the Lord speaks to us, and enlightens, in order to show us the way of salvation. *Your word is a lamp to my feet* (Ps. 118: 105).

St. Bonaventure also says that mental prayer is, as it were, a mirror, in which we see all the stains of the soul. In a letter to the Bishop of Osma, St. Teresa says, "Although it appears to us that we have no imperfections, still when God opens the eyes of the soul, as he usually does in prayer, our imperfections are then clearly seen" (Letter 8). He who does not make mental prayer does not even know his defects, and therefore, as St. Bernard says, he does not abhor them (*De Consid.* l. 1, c. 2). He does not even know the dangers to which his eternal salvation is exposed, and, therefore, he does not even think of avoiding them. But he who applies himself to meditation instantly sees his faults, and the dangers of perdition, and, seeing them, he will reflect on the remedies for them. By meditating on eternity, David was excited to the practice of virtue, and to sorrow and works of penance for his sins. *I thought upon the days of old, and I had in my mind the eternal years . . . and I was exercised, and I swept my spirit* (Ps. 76:6). The spouse in the Canticles says, *The flowers have appeared in our land: the time of pruning is come: the voice of the turtle is heard in our land* (Cant. 2:12). When the soul, like the solitary turtle, retires and recollects itself in meditation to converse with God, then the flowers — that is, good desires — appear: then comes the time of pruning, that is, the correction of faults which are discovered in mental prayer. "Consider," says St. Bernard, "that the time of pruning is at hand, if the time of meditation has gone before" (*De Consid.* l. 2, c. 6). For (says the saint in another place) meditation regulates the affections, directs the actions, and corrects defects (*De Consid.* l. 1, c. 7).

2. IT DISPOSES THE HEART TO PRACTICE VIRTUES

Moreover, without meditation there is not strength to resist the temptations of our enemies, and to practice the virtues of the Gospel.

Meditation is like fire with regard to iron, which, when cold, is hard, and can be wrought only with difficulty. But placed in the fire it becomes soft, and the workman gives it any form he wishes (*De grad. Doctr. Spir.* c. 26), says the venerable Bartholomew à Martyribus. To observe the divine precepts and counsels, it is necessary to have a tender heart, that is, a heart docile and prepared to receive the impressions of celestial inspirations, and ready to obey them. It was this that Solomon asked of God: *Give, therefore, to your servant an understanding heart* (3 Kings 3:9). Sin has made our heart hard and indocile; for, being altogether inclined to sensual pleasures, it resists, as the Apostle complained, the laws of the spirit: *But I see another law in my members, fighting against the law of my mind* (Rom. 7:23). But man becomes docile and tender to the influence of grace which is communicated in mental prayer. By the contemplation of the divine goodness, the great love which God has borne him, and the immense benefits which God has bestowed upon him, man is inflamed with love, his heart is softened, and made obedient to the divine inspirations. But without mental prayer, his heart will remain hard and restive and disobedient, and thus he will be lost: *A hard heart shall fear evil at the last* (Ecclus. 3:27). Hence, St. Bernard exhorted Pope Eugene never to omit meditations on account of external occupations. "I fear for you, O Eugene, lest the multitude of affairs (prayer and consideration being intermitted) may bring you to a hard heart, which abhors not itself, because it perceives not" (*De Consid.* l. 1, c. 2).

Some may imagine that the long time which devout souls give to prayer, and which they could spend in useful works, is unprofitable and lost time. But such persons know not that in mental prayer souls acquire strength to conquer enemies and to practice virtue. "From this leisure," says St. Bernard, "strength comes forth" (*Ex hoc otio vires proveniunt*). Hence, the Lord commanded that his spouse should not be disturbed. *I adjure you . . . that you stir not up, nor awake my beloved till she please* (Cant. 3:5). He says, *until she please*; for the sleep or repose which the soul takes in mental prayer is perfectly voluntary, but is, at the same time, necessary for its spiritual life. He who does not sleep has not strength to work nor to walk, but goes tottering along the way. The soul that does not repose and acquire strength in meditation is not able to resist temptations, and totters on the road. In the life of the Venerable Sister Mary Crucified, we read that, while at prayer, she heard a devil boasting that he had made a nun omit the common meditation, and that afterwards, because he continued to tempt to her, she was in danger of consenting to mortal sin. The servant of God ran to the nun, and, with the divine aid, rescued her from the criminal suggestion. Behold the danger to which one who omits meditation exposes his soul! St. Teresa used to say that he who neglects mental prayer, needs not a devil to carry him to hell, but that he brings himself there with his own hands. And the Abbot Diocles says that "the man who omits mental prayer soon becomes either a beast or a devil."

3. IT HELPS US TO PRAY AS WE SHOULD

Without petitions on our part, God does not grant the divine helps; and without aid from God, we cannot observe the commandments. From the absolute necessity of the prayer of petition arises the moral necessity of mental prayer; for he who neglects meditation, and is distracted with worldly affairs, will not know his spiritual wants, the dangers to which his salvation is exposed, the means which he must adopt in order to conquer temptations, or even the necessity of the prayer of petition for all men; thus, he will give up the practice of prayer, and by neglecting to ask God's graces he will certainly be lost. The great Bishop Palafox, in his Annotations to the letters of St. Teresa, says (Letter 8): "How can charity last, unless God gives perseverance? How will the

Lord give us perseverance, if we neglect to ask him for it? And how shall we ask him without mental prayer? Without mental prayer, there is not the communication with God which is necessary for the preservation of virtue." And Cardinal Bellarmine says, that for him who neglects meditation it is morally impossible to live without sin.

Some one may say, I do not make mental prayer, but I say many vocal prayers. But it is necessary to know, as St. Augustine remarks, that to obtain the divine grace it is not enough to pray with the tongue, it is necessary also to pray with the heart. On the words of David, *I cried to the Lord with my voice* (Ps. 141:2), the holy Doctor says, "Many cry not with their own voice (that is, not with the interior voice of the soul), but with that of the body. Your thoughts are a cry to the Lord (*Enarr. in Ps.* 141). Cry within, where God hears" (*in Ps.* 30. en. 4). This is what the Apostle inculcates: *Praying at all times in the spirit* (Eph. 6:18). In general, vocal prayers are said distractedly with the voice of the body, but not of the heart, especially when they are long, and still more especially when said by a person who does not make mental prayer; and, therefore, God seldom hears them, and seldom grants the graces asked. Many say the Rosary, the Office of the Blessed Virgin, and perform other works of

71

devotion; but they still continue in sin. But it is impossible for him who perseveres in mental prayer to continue in sin: he will either give up meditation or renounce sin. A great servant of God used to say that mental prayer and sin cannot exist together. And this we see by experience: they who make mental prayer rarely incur the enmity of God; and should they ever have the misfortune of falling into sin, by persevering in mental prayer they see their misery and return to God. Let a soul, says St. Teresa, be ever so negligent, if it persevere in meditation, the Lord will bring it back to the haven of salvation.

II

Indispensable to Attain Perfection

ALL the saints have become saints by mental prayer. Mental prayer is the blessed furnace in which souls are inflamed with the divine love. *In my meditation*, says David, *a fire shall flame out* (Ps. 38:4). St. Vincent of Paul used to say that it would be a miracle if a sinner who attends at the sermons in the mission, or in the spiritual exercises, were not converted. Now, he who preaches, and speaks in the exercises, is only a man; but it is God himself that speaks to the soul in meditation. *I will lead her into the wilderness; and I will speak to her heart* (Osee 2:14). St. Catherine of Bologna used to say, "He who does not practice mental prayer deprives himself of the bond that unites the soul with God; hence, finding her alone, the devil will easily make her his own." "How," she would say, "can I conceive that the love of God is found in the soul that cares but little to treat with God in prayer?"

Where, but in meditation, have the saints been inflamed with divine love? By means of mental prayer, St. Peter of Alcantara was inflamed to such a degree that in order to cool himself, he ran into a frozen pool, and the frozen water began to boil like water in a caldron placed on the fire. In mental prayer, St. Philip Neri became inflamed, and trembled so that he shook the entire room. In mental prayer, St. Aloysius Gonzaga was so inflamed with divine ardor that his very face appeared to be on fire, and his heart beat as strongly as if it wished to fly from the body.

St. Laurence Justinian says: "By the efficacy of mental prayer, temptation is banished, sadness is driven away, lost virtue is restored, fervor which has grown cold is excited, and the lovely flame of divine love is augmented" (*De Casto Conn.* c. 22). Hence, St. Aloysius Gonzaga has justly said that he who does not make much mental prayer will never attain a high degree of perfection.

A man of prayer, says David, is like a tree planted near the current of waters, which brings forth fruit in due time; all his actions prosper before God. *Blessed is the man . . . who shall meditate on his law day and night! And he shall be like a tree which is planted near the running waters, which shall bring forth its fruit in due season, and his leaf shall not fall off: and all whatsoever he shall do shall prosper* (Ps. 1:3). Mark the words *in due season*; that is, at the time when he ought to bear such a pain, such an affront, etc.

St. John Chrysostom (*Ad pop. Ant. hom.* 79) compared mental prayer to a fountain in the middle of a garden. Oh! what an abundance of flowers and verdant plants do we see in the garden which is always refreshed with water from the fountain! Such, precisely, is the soul that practices mental prayer: you will see, that it always advances in good desires, and that it always brings forth more abundant fruits of virtue. From where does the soul receive so many blessings? From meditation, by which it is continually irrigated. *Your plants are a paradise of pomegranates with the fruits of the orchard . . . The fountain of gardens, the well of living waters, which run with a strong stream from Libanus* (Cant. 4:13). But let the fountain cease to water the garden, and, behold, the flowers, plants, and all instantly wither away; and why? Because the water has failed. You will see that as long as such a person makes mental prayer, he is modest, humble, devout, and mortified in all things. But let him omit meditation, and you will instantly find him wanting in modesty of the eyes, proud, resenting every word, indevout, no longer frequenting the sacraments and the church; you will find him attached to vanity, to useless conversations, to pastimes, and to earthly pleasures; and why? The water has failed, and, therefore, fervor has ceased. *My soul is as earth without water unto you . . . My spirit has fainted away* (Ps. 142:6). The soul has neglected mental prayer, the garden is therefore dried up, and the miserable soul goes from bad to worse. When a soul abandons meditation, St. Chrysostom regards it not only as sick, but as dead. "He," says the holy Doctor, "who prays not to God, nor desires to enjoy assiduously his divine conversation, is dead . . . The death of the soul is not to be prostrated before God" (*De or. D.* l. 1).

The same Father says that mental prayer is the root of the fruitful vine (*De or. D.* l. 1). And St. John Climacus writes, that "prayer is a bulwark against the assault of afflictions, the spring of virtues, the procurer of graces" (*Scal. par.* gr. 28). Rufinus asserts, that all the spiritual progress of the soul flows from mental prayer (*in Ps.* 36). And Gerson goes so far as to say that he who neglects meditation cannot, without a miracle, lead the life of a Christian (*De Med. cons.* 7). Speaking of mental prayer, Jeremias says, *He shall sit solitary, and hold his peace; because he has taken it up upon himself* (Lam. 3:28). That is, a soul cannot have a relish for God, unless it withdraws from creatures, and *sits*, that is, stops to contemplate the goodness, the love, the amiableness of God. But when solitary and recollected in meditation—that is, when it takes away its thoughts from the world—it is then raised above itself; and departs from prayer very different from what it was when it began it.

St. Ignatius of Loyola used to say that mental prayer is the short way to attain perfection. In a word, he who advances most in meditation makes the greatest progress in perfection. In mental prayer the soul is filled with holy thoughts, with holy affections, desires, and holy resolutions, and with love for God. There man sacrifices his passions, his appetites, his earthly attachments, and all the interests of self-love. Moreover, by praying for them, in mental prayer, we can save many sinners, as was done by St. Teresa, St. Mary Magdalene de Pazzi, and is done by all souls enamored of God, who never omit, in their meditations, to recommend to him all infidels, heretics, and all poor sinners; begging him also to give zeal to priests who work in his vineyard, that they may convert his enemies. In mental prayer we can also, by the sole desire of performing them, gain the merit of many good works which we do not perform. For, as the Lord punishes bad desires, so, on the other hand, he rewards all our good desires.

PRAYER

My Jesus, You have loved me in the midst of pains; and in the midst of sufferings, I wish to love You. You have spared nothing, You have even given Your blood and Your life, in order to gain my love; and shall I continue, as before, to be reserved in loving You? No, my Redeemer, it shall not be so: the ingratitude with which I have previously treated You is sufficient. To You I consecrate my whole heart. You alone do deserve all my love. You alone do I wish to love. My God, since You wish me to be entirely Yours, give me strength to serve You as You deserve, during the remainder of my life. Pardon my tepidity and my past infidelities. How often have I omitted mental prayer, in order to indulge my caprice! Alas! how often, when it was in my power to remain with You in order to please You, have I remained with creatures, so as to offend You! Oh, that so many lost years would return! But, since they will not return, the remaining days of my life must be entirely Yours, O my beloved Lord! I love You, O my Jesus! I love You, O my Sovereign Good! You are and shall be forever the only love of my soul. O Mother of fair love, O Mary! obtain for me the grace to love your Son, and to spend the remainder of my life in his love. You do obtain from Jesus whatsoever you wish. Through your prayer I hope for this gift.

III

The Ends of Mental Prayer

IN order to practice well mental prayer, or meditation, and to make it truly profitable to the soul, we must well ascertain the ends for which we attempt it.

1. TO UNITE OURSELVES TO GOD

We must meditate in order to unite ourselves more completely to God. It is not so much good thoughts in the intellect as good acts of the will, or holy desires, that unite us to God; and such are the acts which we perform in meditation — acts of humility, confidence, self-sacrifice, resignation, and especially of love and of repentance for our sins. Acts of love, says St. Teresa, are those that keep the soul inflamed with holy love.

But the perfection of this love consists in making our will one with that of God; for the chief effect of love, as Dionysius the Areopagite says, is to unite the wills of those who love, so that they have but one heart and one will. St. Teresa also says, "All that he who exercises himself in prayer should aim at, is to conform himself to the divine will, and he may be assured that in this consists the highest perfection; he who best practices this will receive the greatest gifts from God, and will make the greatest progress in an interior life" (*Interior Castle* d. 2, ch. 1).

There are many, however, who complain that they go to prayer and do not find God; the reason of which is, that they carry with them a heart full of earth. "Detach the heart from creatures, says St. Teresa; seek God, and you will find him." *The Lord is good to the soul that seeks Him* (Lam. 3:25). Therefore, to find God in prayer, the soul must be stripped of its love for the things of earth, and then God will speak to it: *I will lead her into the wilderness, and I will speak to her heart* (Osee 2:14). But in order to find God, solitude of the body, as St. Gregory observes, is not enough; that of the heart is necessary too. The Lord one day said to St. Teresa: "I would willingly speak to many souls; but the world makes such a noise in their heart that my voice cannot make itself heard." Ah! when a detached soul is engaged in prayer, truly does God speak to it, and make it understand the love which he has borne it; and then the soul, says St. Laurence Justinian, burning with holy love, speaks not; but in that silence, oh, how much does it say! The silence of charity, observes the same writer, says more to God than could be said by the utmost powers of human eloquence; each sigh that it utters is a manifestation of its whole interior

(*De Disc. mon.* c. 24). It then seems as if it could not repeat often enough, *My Beloved to me, and I to Him.*

2. TO OBTAIN GRACE FROM GOD

We must meditate in order to obtain from God the graces that are necessary to advance in the way of salvation, and especially to avoid sin, and to use the means which will lead us to perfection.

The best fruit which comes from meditation is the exercise of prayer. Almighty God, ordinarily speaking, does not give grace to any but those who pray. St. Gregory writes: "God desires to be entreated; he desires to be constrained; he desires to be, as it were, conquered by importunity." It is true that at all times the Lord is ready to hear us, but at the time of meditation, when we are most truly in converse with God, he is most bountiful in giving us his aid.

Above all, should we, in meditation, ask God for perseverance and his holy love.

Final perseverance is not a single grace, but a chain of graces, to which must correspond the chain of our prayers. If we cease to pray, God will cease to give us his help, and we shall perish. He who does not practice meditation will find the greatest difficulty in persevering in grace till death. Let us remember what Palafox says: "How will the Lord give us perseverance if we do not ask it? And how shall we ask for it without meditation? Without meditation there is no communion with God."

We must also be urgent with prayers to obtain from God his holy love. St. Francis de Sales says that all virtues come in union with holy love. *All good things came to me together with her* (Wisd. 7:11).

Let us, therefore, pray continually for perseverance and love; and, in order to pray with greater confidence, let us ever bear in mind the promise made us by Jesus Christ, that whatever we seek from God through the merits of his Son, he will give it us (John 16:23). Let us, then, pray, and pray always, if we would that God should make us abound in every blessing. Let us pray for ourselves, and, if we have zeal for the glory of God, let us pray also for others. It is a thing most pleasing to God to be entreated for unbelievers and heretics, and all sinners. *Let the people, O God, confess to You; let all the people give praise to You* (Ps. 66:6). Let us say, O Lord, make them know You, make them love You. We read in the lives of St. Teresa and St. Mary Magdalene of Pazzi how God inspired these holy women to pray for sinners. And to prayer for sinners let us also add prayers for the holy souls in purgatory.

3. NOT TO SEEK SPIRITUAL CONSOLATIONS

We must apply ourselves to meditation, not for the sake of spiritual consolations, but chiefly in order to learn what is the will of God concerning us. *Speak, Lord*, said Samuel to God, *for Your servant hears* (1 Kings 3:9). Lord, make me to know what You will, that I may do it. Some persons continue meditation as long as consolations continue; but when these cease, they leave off meditation. It is true that God is accustomed to comfort his beloved souls at the time of meditation, and to give them some foretaste of the delights he prepares in heaven for those who love him. These are things which the lovers of the world do not comprehend; they who have no taste except for earthly delights despise those which are celestial. Oh, if they were wise, how surely would they leave their pleasures to shut themselves in their closets, to speak alone with God! Meditation is nothing more than a converse between the soul and God; the soul pours forth to him its affections, its desires, its fears, its requests, and God speaks to the heart, causing it to know his goodness, and the love which he bears it, and what it must do to please him.

But these delights are not constant, and, for the most part, holy souls experience much dryness of spirit in meditation. "With dryness and temptations," says St. Teresa, "the Lord makes proof of those who love him." And she adds, "Even if this dryness lasts through life, let not the soul leave off meditation; the time will come when all will be well rewarded." The time of dryness is the time for gaining the greatest rewards; and when we find ourselves apparently without fervor, without good desires, and, as it were, unable to do a good act, let us humble ourselves and resign ourselves, for this very meditation will be more fruitful than others. It is enough then to say, if we can say nothing more, "O Lord, help me, have mercy on me, abandon me not!" Let us also have recourse to our comforter, the most holy Mary. Happy is he who does not leave off meditation in the hour of desolation.

IV

Principal Subjects of Meditation

THE Holy Spirit says, *In all your works remember your last end, and you shall never sin* (Ecclus. 7:40). He who often meditates on the four last things —namely, death, judgment, and the eternity of hell and paradise—will not fall into sin. But these truths are not seen with the eye of the body; the soul only perceives them. If they are not meditated on, they vanish from the mind; and then the pleasures of the senses present themselves, and those who do not keep before themselves the eternal truths are easily taken up by them; and this is the reason why so many abandon themselves to vice, and are damned. All Christians know and believe that they must die, and that we shall all be judged; but because they do not think about this, they live far away from God.

If we, moreover, do not meditate especially on our obligation to love God on account of his infinite perfections and the great blessings that he has conferred upon us, and the love that he has borne us, we shall hardly detach ourselves from the love of creatures in order to fix our whole love on God. It is in the time of prayer that God gives us to understand the worthlessness of earthly things, and the value of the good things of heaven; and then it is that he inflames with his love those hearts that do not offer resistance to his calls.

After all, the good rule is that we preferably meditate on the truths and mysteries that touch us more and procure for our soul the most abundant nourishment. Yet the subject most suitable for a person that aspires to perfection ought to be the Passion of our Lord. Louis Blosius relates that our Lord revealed to several holy women — St. Gertrude, St. Bridget, St. Mechtilde, and St. Catherine of Sienna — that they who meditate on his Passion are very dear to him. According to St. Francis de Sales, the Passion of our Redeemer should be the ordinary subject of the meditation of every Christian. Oh, what an excellent book is the Passion of Jesus! There we understand, better than in any other book, the malice of sin, and also the mercy and love of God for man. To me it appears that Jesus Christ has suffered so many different pains — the scourging, the crowning with thorns, the crucifixion, etc. — that, having before our eyes so many painful mysteries, we might have a variety of different subjects for meditating on his Passion, by which we might excite sentiments of gratitude and love.

V

The Place and the Time Suitable for Meditation

1. THE PLACE

W E can meditate in every place, at home or elsewhere, even in walking, in working. How many are there who, not being able to do otherwise, raise their hearts to God and apply their minds to mental prayer without leaving for this purpose their occupations, their work, or meditate even when traveling! He who seeks God will find him everywhere and at all times.

The essential condition to converse with God is the solitude of the heart, without which prayer would be worthless, and, as St. Gregory says, it would profit us little or nothing to be with the body in a solitary place, while the heart is full of worldly thoughts and affections (*Mor.* l. 30, c. 23). But to enjoy the solitude of the heart, which consists in being disengaged from worldly thoughts and affections, deserts and caves are not absolutely necessary. Those who from necessity are obliged to converse with the world, whenever their hearts are free from worldly attachments, even in the public streets, in places of resort, and public assemblies, can possess a solitude of heart, and continue united with God. All those occupations that we undertake in order to fulfill the divine will have no power to prevent the solitude of the heart. St. Catherine of Sienna truly found God in the midst of the household labors in which her parents kept her employed in order to draw her from devotional exercises; but in the midst of these affairs she preserved a retirement in her heart, which she called her cell, and there ceased not to converse with God alone.

However, when we can, we should retire to a solitary place to make our meditation. Our Lord has said, *When you shall pray, enter your chamber, and, having shut the door, pray to your Father in secret* (Matt. 6:6). St. Bernard says that silence, and the absence of all noise, almost force the soul to think of the goods of heaven (*Epist.* 78).

But the best place for making mental prayer is the church; for Jesus Christ especially delights in the meditation that is made before the Blessed Sacrament, since there it appears that he bestows light and grace most abundantly upon those who visit him. He has left himself in this sacrament, not only to be the food of souls that receive him in Holy Communion, but also to be found at all times by every one who seeks him. Devout pilgrims go to the holy town of Loreto, where Jesus Christ dwelt during his life; and to Jerusalem, where he died on the cross; but how much greater ought to be our devotion when we find him before us in the tabernacle, in which this Lord himself now dwells in person, who lived among us, and died for us on Calvary! It is not permitted in the world for persons of all ranks to speak alone with kings; but with Jesus Christ, the King of kings, both nobles and plebeians, rich and poor, can converse at their will, setting before him their wants, and seeking his grace; and there Jesus gives audience to all, hears all, and comforts all.

2. THE TIME

We have here to consider two things — namely, the time of the day most suitable for mental prayer, and the time to be spent in making it.

1. According to St. Bonaventure, the morning and the evening are the two parts of the day which, ordinarily speaking, are the fittest for meditation (*Spec. disc.* p. 1, c. 12). But, according to St. Gregory of Nyssa, the morning is the most seasonable time for prayer, because, says the saint, when prayer precedes business, sin will not find entrance into the soul (*De orat. Dom.* or. 1). And the Venerable Father Charles Carafa, founder of the Congregation of the *Pious Workers*, used to say that a fervent act of love, made in the morning

during meditation, is sufficient to maintain the soul in fervor during the entire day. Prayer, as St. Jerome has written, is also necessary in the evening. Let not the body go to rest before the soul is refreshed by mental prayer (*Ad Eust. de Virgin*), which is the food of the soul. But at all times and in all places we can pray; it is enough for us to raise the mind to God, and to make good acts, for in this consists mental prayer.

2. With regard to the time to be spent in mental prayer, the rule of the saints was, to devote to it all the hours that were not necessary for the occupations of human life. St. Francis Borgia employed in meditation eight hours in the day, because his Superiors would not allow him a longer time; and when the eight hours had expired, he earnestly asked permission to remain a little longer at prayer, saying, "Ah! give me another little quarter of an hour." St. Philip Neri was accustomed to spend the entire night in prayer. St. Anthony the Abbot remained the whole night in prayer; and when the sun appeared, which was the time assigned for terminating his prayer, he complained of it for having risen too soon.

Father Balthasar Alvarez used to say that a soul that loves God, when not in prayer, is like a stone out of its centre, in a violent state; for in this life we should, as much as possible, imitate the life of the saints in bliss, who are constantly employed in the contemplation of God.

But let us come to the particular time which a religious who seeks perfection should devote to mental prayer. Father Torres prescribed an hour's meditation in the morning, another during the day, and a half-hour's meditation in the evening, when they should not be hindered by sickness, or by any duty of obedience. If to you this appears too much, I counsel you to give at least two hours to mental prayer. It is certain that a half-hour's meditation each day would not be sufficient to attain a high degree of perfection; for beginners, however, this would be sufficient.

Sometimes the Lord wishes you to omit prayer in order to perform some work of fraternal charity; but it is necessary to attend to what St. Laurence Justinian says: "When charity requires it, the spouse of Jesus goes to serve her neighbor; but during that time she continually sighs to return to converse with her Spouse in the solitude of her cell" (*De Casto Conn.* c. 12). Father Vincent Carafa, General of the Society of Jesus, stole as many little moments of time as he could, and employed them in prayer.

Mental prayer is tedious to those who are attached to the world, but not to those who love God only. Ah! conversation with God is not painful nor tedious to those who truly love him. *His conversation has no bitterness, his company produces not tediousness, but joy and gladness* (Wisd. 8:16). Mental prayer, says St. John Climacus, is nothing else than a familiar conversation and union with God (*Scal. par.* gr. 28). In prayer, as St. Chrysostom says, the soul converses with God, and God with the soul. No, the life of holy persons who love prayer, and fly from earthly amusements, is not a life of bitterness. If you do not believe me, *Taste and see that the Lord is sweet* (Ps. 33:9). Try it, and you shall see how sweet the Lord is to those who leave all things in order to converse with him only. But the end which we ought to propose to ourselves in going to meditation should be, as has been said several times, not spiritual consolation, but to learn from our Lord what he wishes from us, and to divest ourselves of all self-love. "To prepare yourself for prayer," says St. John Climacus, "put off your own will" (*Ad præparandum te ad orationem, exue voluntates tuas*). To prepare ourselves well for meditation, we must renounce self-will, and say to God, *Speak, Lord, for your servant hears* (1 Kings 3:10). Lord, tell me what You wish me to do; I am willing to do it. And it is necessary to say this with a resolute will, for without this disposition the Lord will not speak to us.

VI

Manner of Making Mental Prayer

MENTAL prayer contains three parts: the preparation, the meditation, and the conclusion.

1. THE PREPARATION

Begin by disposing your mind and body to enter into pious recollection.

Leave at the door of the place where you are going to converse with God all extraneous thoughts, saying, with St. Bernard, O my thoughts! wait here: after prayer we shall speak on other matters. Be careful not to allow the mind to wander where it wishes; but should a distracting thought enter, act as we shall tell you to do in § VII.

The posture of the body most suitable for prayer is to be kneeling; but if this posture becomes so irksome as to cause distractions, we may, as St. John of the Cross says, make our meditation while modestly sitting down.

The preparation consists of three acts: 1. Act of faith in the presence of God; 2. Act of humility and of contrition; 3. Act of petition for light. We may perform these acts in the following manner:

Mental Prayer

Act of Faith in the Presence of God, and Act of Adoration

My God, I believe that You are here present, and I adore You with my whole soul.

Be careful to make this act with a lively faith, for a lively remembrance of the divine presence contributes greatly to remove distractions. Cardinal Carracciolo, Bishop of Aversa, used to say that when a person is distracted in prayer there is reason to think that he has not made a lively act of faith.

Act of Humility and of Contrition

Lord, I should now be in hell in punishment of the offences I have given You. I am sorry for them from the bottom of my heart; have mercy on me.

Act of Petition for Light

Eternal Father, for the sake of Jesus and Mary, give me light in this meditation, that I may draw fruit from it.

We must then recommend ourselves to the Blessed Virgin by saying a *Hail Mary*, to St. Joseph, to our guardian angel, and to our holy patron.

These acts, says St. Francis de Sales, ought to be made with fervor, but should be short, that we may pass immediately to the meditation.

2. THE MEDITATION

When you make meditation privately you may always use some pious book, at least at the commencement, and stop when you find yourself most touched. St. Francis de Sales says that in this we should do as the bees that stop on a flower as long as they find any honey on it, and then pass on to another. St. Teresa used a book for seventeen years; she would first read a little, then meditate for a short time on what she had read. It is useful to meditate in this manner, in imitation of the pigeon that first drinks and then raises its eyes to heaven.

When mental prayer is made in common, one person reads for the rest the subject of meditation and divides it into two parts: the first is read at the beginning, after the preparatory acts; the second, towards the middle of the half hour, or after the Consecration if the meditation is made during the

Mass. One should read in a loud tone of voice, and slowly, so as to be well understood.

It should be remembered that the advantage of mental prayer consists not so much in meditating as in making affections, petitions, and resolutions: these are the three principal fruits of meditation. "The progress of a soul," says St. Teresa, "does not consist in thinking much of God, but in loving him ardently; and this love is acquired by resolving to do a great deal for him" (*Book of the Foundations* ch. 5). Speaking of mental prayer, the spiritual masters say that meditation is, as it were, the needle which, when it has passed, must be succeeded by the golden thread, composed, as has been said, of affections, petitions, and resolutions; and this we are going to explain.

The Affections

When you have reflected on the point of meditation, and feel any pious sentiment, raise your heart to God and offer him acts of humility, of confidence, or of thanksgiving; but, above all, repeat in mental prayer acts of contrition and of love.

The act of love, as also the act of contrition, is the golden chain that binds the soul to God. An act of perfect charity is sufficient for the remission

of all our sins: *Charity covers a multitude of sins*
(1 Peter 4:8). The Lord has declared that he cannot
hate the soul that loves him: *I love them that love Me*
(Prov. 8:17). The Venerable Sister Mary Crucified
once saw a globe of fire, in which some straws that
had been thrown into it were instantly consumed.
By this vision she was given to understand that a
soul, by making a true act of love, obtains the
remission of all its faults. Besides, the Angelic
Doctor teaches that by every act of love we acquire
a new degree of glory. "Every act of charity merits
eternal life" (*Summa Theol.* 1. 2. q. 114, a. 7).

Acts of love may be made in the following
manner:

My God, I esteem You more than all things.
I love You with my whole heart.
I delight in Your felicity.
I would wish to see You loved by all.
I wish only what You wish.
Make known to me what You wish from
me, and I will do it.
Dispose as You please of me and of all that I
possess.

This last act of oblation is particularly dear to
God.

In meditation, among the acts of love towards God, there is none more perfect than the taking delight in the infinite joy of God. This is certainly the continual exercise of the blessed in heaven; so that he who often rejoices in the joy of God begins in this life to do that which he hopes to do in heaven through all eternity.

It may be useful here to remark, with St. Augustine, that it is not the torture, but the cause, which makes the martyr (*Epist.* 89 E. B.). Accordingly, St. Thomas (*Summa Theol.* 2. 2. q. 124, a. 5) teaches that martyrdom is to suffer death in the exercise of an act of virtue. From which we may infer, that not only he who by the hands of the executioner lays down his life for the faith, but whoever dies to comply with the divine will, and to please God, is a martyr, since in sacrificing himself to the divine love he performs an act of the most exalted virtue. We all have to pay the great debt of nature; let us therefore endeavor, in holy prayer, to obtain resignation to the divine will—to receive death and every tribulation in conformity with the dispensations of his Providence. As often as we shall perform this act of resignation with sufficient fervor, we may hope to be made partakers of the merits of the martyrs. St. Mary Magdalene, in reciting the doxology, always bowed her head in the same spirit as she would have done in receiving the stroke of the executioner.

Remember that we here speak of the ordinary mental prayer; for should any one feel himself at any time united with God by supernatural or infused recollection, without any particular thought of an eternal truth or of any divine mystery, he should not then labor to perform any other acts than those to which he feels himself sweetly drawn to God. It is then enough to endeavor, with loving attention, to remain united with God, without impeding the divine operation, or forcing himself to make reflections and acts. But this is to be understood when the Lord calls the soul to this supernatural prayer; but until we receive such a call, we should not depart from the ordinary method of mental prayer, but should, as has been said, make use of meditation and affections. However, for persons accustomed to mental prayer, it is better to employ themselves in affections than in consideration.

Petitions

Moreover, in mental prayer it is very profitable, and perhaps more useful than any other act, to repeat petitions to God, asking, with humility and confidence, his graces; that is, his light, resignation, perseverance, and the like; but, above all, the gift of his holy love. St. Francis de Sales used to say that by obtaining the divine love we obtain all graces; for a soul that truly loves God with its whole heart will, of itself, without being admonished by others, abstain from giving him the smallest displeasure, and will labor to please him to the best of its ability.

When you find yourself in aridity and darkness, so that you feel, as it were, incapable of making good acts, it is sufficient to say:

My Jesus, mercy. Lord, for the sake of Your mercy, assist me.

And the meditation made in this manner will be for you perhaps the most useful and fruitful.

The Venerable Paul Segneri used to say that until he studied theology, he employed himself during the time of mental prayer in making reflections and affections; but "God" (these are his own words) "afterwards opened my eyes, and thenceforward I endeavored to employ myself in petitions; and if there is any good in me, I ascribe it to this exercise of recommending myself to God." Do you likewise do the same; ask of God his graces, in the name of Jesus Christ, and you will obtain whatsoever you desire. This our Savior has promised, and his promise cannot fail:

Manner of Making Mental Prayer

Amen, amen, I say to you, if you ask the Father anything in My name, He will give it you.

In a word, all mental prayer should consist in acts and petitions. Hence, the Venerable Sister Mary Crucified, while in an ecstasy, declared that mental prayer is the respiration of the soul; for, as by respiration, the air is first attracted, and afterwards given back, so, by petitions, the soul first receives grace from God, and then, by good acts of oblation and love, it gives itself to him.

Resolutions

In terminating the meditation it is necessary to make a particular resolution; as, for example, to avoid some particular defect into which you have more frequently fallen, or to practice some virtue, such as to suffer the annoyance which you receive from another person, to obey more exactly a certain Superior, to perform some particular act of mortification. We must repeat the same resolution several times, until we find that we have got rid of the defect or acquired the virtue. Afterwards reduce to practice the resolutions you have made, as soon as an occasion is presented. You would also do well, before the conclusion of your prayer, to renew the vows or any particular engagement by vow or otherwise that you have made with

God. This renewal is most pleasing to God; we multiply the merit of the good work, and draw down upon us a new help in order to persevere and to grow in grace.

3. THE CONCLUSION

The conclusion of meditation consists of three acts:

1. In thanking God for the lights received.
2. In making a purpose to fulfill the resolutions made.
3. In asking of the Eternal Father, for the sake of Jesus and Mary, grace to be faithful to them.

Be careful never to omit, at the end of meditation, to recommend to God the souls in purgatory and poor sinners. St. John Chrysostom says that nothing more clearly shows our love for Jesus Christ than our zeal in recommending our brethren to him.

St. Francis de Sales remarks that in leaving mental prayer we should take with us a nosegay of flowers, in order to smell them during the day; that is, we should remember one or two points in which we have felt particular devotion, in order to excite our fervor during the day.

Manner of Making Mental Prayer

The ejaculations which are dearest to God are those of love, of resignation, of oblation of ourselves. Let us endeavor not to perform any action without first offering it to God, and not to allow at the most a quarter of an hour to pass, in whatever occupations we may find ourselves, without raising the heart to the Lord by some good act. Moreover, in our leisure time, such as when we are waiting for a person, or when we walk in the garden, or are confined to bed by sickness, let us endeavor, to the best of our ability, to unite ourselves to God. It is also necessary by observing silence, by seeking solitude as much as possible, and by remembering the presence of God, to preserve the pious sentiments conceived in meditation.

VII

Distractions and Aridities

1. DISTRACTIONS

IF, after having well prepared ourselves for mental prayer, as has been explained in a preceding paragraph, a distracting thought should enter, we must not be disturbed, nor seek to banish it with a violent effort; but let us remove it calmly and return to God.

Let us remember that the devil labors hard to disturb us in the time of meditation, in order to make us abandon it. Let him, then, who omits mental prayer on account of distractions, be persuaded that he gives delight to the devil. It is impossible, says Cassian, that our minds should be free from all distractions during prayer.

Let us, then, never give up meditation, however great our distractions may be. St. Francis de Sales says that if, in mental prayer, we should do nothing else than continually banish distractions and temptations, the meditation would be well made. Before him St. Thomas taught that involuntary distractions do not take away the fruit of mental prayer (*Summa Theol.* 2. 2. q. 83, a. 13).

Finally, when we perceive that we are deliberately distracted, let us desist from the voluntary defect and banish the distraction, but let us be careful not to discontinue our meditation.

2. ARIDITIES

The greatest pain of souls in meditation is to find themselves sometimes without a feeling of devotion, weary of it, and without any sensible desire of loving God; and with this is joined the fear of being in the wrath of God through their sins, on account of which the Lord has abandoned them; and being in this gloomy darkness, they know not how to escape from it, it seeming to them that every way is closed against them.

When a soul gives itself up to the spiritual life, the Lord is accustomed to heap consolations upon it, in order to wean it from the pleasures of the world, but afterwards, when he sees it more settled in spiritual ways, he draws back his hand, in order to make proof of its love, and to see whether it serves and loves God unrecompensed, while in this world, with spiritual joys. Some foolish persons, seeing themselves in a state of aridity, think that God may have abandoned them; or, again, that the spiritual life was not made for them; and so they leave off prayer, and lose all that they have gained.

In order to be a soul of prayer, man must resist with fortitude all temptations to discontinue mental prayer in the time of aridity. St. Teresa has left us very excellent instructions on this point. In one place she says, "The devil knows that he has lost the soul that perseveringly practices mental prayer." In another place she says, "I hold for certain that the Lord will conduct to the haven of salvation the soul that perseveres in mental prayer, in spite of all the sins that the devil may oppose." Again, she says, "He who does not stop in the way of mental prayer reaches the end of his journey, though he should delay a little." Finally she concludes, saying, "By aridity and temptations the Lord proves his lovers. Though aridity should last for life, let not the soul give up prayer: the time will come when all shall be well rewarded."

The Angelic Doctor says that the devotion consists not in feeling, but in the desire and resolution to embrace promptly all that God wills. Such was the prayer that Jesus Christ made in the Garden of Olives; it was full of aridity and tediousness, but it was the most devout and meritorious prayer that had ever been offered in this world. It consisted in these words: My Father, not what I will, but what You will.

Hence, never give up mental prayer in the time of aridity. Should the tediousness which assails you be very great, divide your meditation into several parts, and employ yourself, for the most part, in petitions to God, even though you should seem to pray without confidence and without fruit. It will be sufficient to say and to repeat: *My Jesus, mercy. Lord, have mercy on us.* Pray, and doubt not that God will hear you and grant your petition.

In going to meditation, never propose to yourself your own pleasure and satisfaction, but only to please God, and to learn what he wishes you to do. And, for this purpose, pray always that God may make known to you his will, and that he may give you strength to fulfill it. All that we ought to seek in mental prayer is, light to know, and strength to accomplish, the will of God in our regard.

PRAYER

Ah! my Jesus, it appears that You could do nothing more, in order to gain the love of men. It is enough to know that You have wished to become man; that is, to become, like us, a worm. You have wished to lead a painful life, of thirty-three years, amid sorrow and ignominies, and in the end to die on an infamous gibbet. You have also wished to remain under the appearance of bread, in order to become the food of our souls; and how is it possible that You have received so much ingratitude, even from Christians who believe these truths, and still love You so little? Unhappy me! I have once been among those ungrateful souls; I have attended only to my pleasures, and have been forgetful of You and of Your love. I now know the evil I have done; but I repent of it with my whole heart: my Jesus, pardon me. I now love You; I love You so ardently that I choose death, and a thousand deaths, rather than cease to love You. I thank You for the light which You give me. Give me strength, O God of my soul! always to advance in Your love. Accept this poor heart to love You. It is true that it has once despised You, but now it is enamored of Your goodness; it loves You and desires only to love You. O Mary, mother of God, assist me: in your intercession I place great confidence.

THE PRESENCE OF GOD

THE PRESENCE OF GOD

I

Effects Produced by This Holy Exercise

THE practice of the presence of God is justly called by spiritual masters the foundation of a spiritual life, which consists in three things: the avoidance of sin, the practice of virtue, and union with God. These three effects the presence of God produces: it preserves the soul from sin, leads it to the practice of virtue, and moves it to unite itself to God by means of holy love.

1. THE AVOIDANCE OF SIN

As to the first effect, the avoidance of sin, there is no more efficacious means of subduing the passions, resisting temptations, and consequently of avoiding sin, than the remembrance of God's presence. The angelic Doctor says: "If we always thought that God was looking at us, we would never, or scarcely ever, do what is displeasing in his eyes" (*Opusc.* 58, c. 2). And St. Jerome has written that the remembrance of God's presence closes the door against all sins. "The remembrance of God," says the holy Doctor, "shuts out all sins" (in *Ezech.* c. 22). And if men will not dare in their presence to transgress the commands of princes, parents, or Superiors, how could they ever violate the laws of God if they thought that he was looking at them? St. Ambrose relates that a page of Alexander the Great, who held in his hand a lighted torch while Alexander was offering sacrifice in the temple, suffered his hand to be burnt sooner than be guilty of irreverence by allowing the torch to fall. The saint adds (*De Virgin.* l. 3), that if reverence to his sovereign could conquer nature in a boy, how much more will the thought of the divine presence make a faithful soul overcome every temptation, and suffer every pain rather than insult the Lord before his face!

All the sins of men flow from their losing sight of the divine presence. "Every evil," says St. Teresa, "happens to us because we do not reflect that God is present with us, but imagine that he is at a distance" (*Way of Perf.* ch. 29). And before her David said the same: *God is not before his eyes; his ways are filthy at all times* (Ps. 9:26). Sinners forget that God sees them, and therefore they offend him at all times. The Abbot Diocles went so far as to say (*Pallad. Hist. Laus.* c. 98) that "he who distracts himself from the remembrance of the presence of God becomes either a beast or a devil." And justly; for he shall be instantly assailed by carnal or diabolical desires which he will not have strength to resist.

On the other hand, the saints by the thought that God was looking at them have bravely repelled all the assaults of their enemies. This thought gave courage to holy Susanna to resist the temptations of the Elders, and even to despise their threats against her life. Hence she courageously said to them: *It is better for me to fall into your hands without doing it than to sin in the sight of the Lord* (Dan. 13:23). It is better to fall into your hands and to die without sin than to offend God before his face. This thought also converted a wicked woman who dared to tempt St. Ephrem; the saint told her that if she wished to sin she must meet him in the middle of the city. But, said she, how is it possible to commit sin before so many persons? And how, replied the saint, is it possible to sin in the presence of God, who sees us in every place? At these words she burst into tears, and falling prostrate on the ground asked pardon of the saint, and besought him to point out to her the way of salvation. St. Ephrem placed her in a monastery, where she led a holy life, weeping over her sins till death (*Metaphrast. Vit. S. Ephrem*).

The Presence of God

The same happened to the abbot Paphnutius and a sinner called Thais. She tempted him one day, saying that there was no one to see them but God. The saint with a stern voice said to her: "Then you believe that God sees you, and will you commit sin?" Thais was thunderstruck, and filled with horror for her sinful life: she gathered together all her riches, clothes, and jewels which she had earned by her infamous practices, burned them in the public square, and retired into a monastery, where she fasted on bread and water every day for three successive years, always repeating this prayer: "O You who have made me, have mercy on me! (*Qui plasmasti me, miserere mei*). My God, who have created me, have pity on me!" After these three years she happily ended her life by a holy death. It was afterwards revealed to Paul, a disciple of St. Anthony, that this happy penitent was placed among the saints on an exalted throne of glory (*Vit. Patr.* l. 1).

Behold the efficacy of the remembrance of the divine presence to make us avoid sins. Let us then always pray to the Lord, saying with Job: *Set me beside you, and let any man's hand fight against me* (Job 17:3). My God, place me in Your presence; that is, remind me in every place that You see me, and then let all my enemies assail me: I shall always defeat them. Hence St. Chrysostom concludes: "If we keep ourselves always in the

114

presence of God, the thought that he sees all our thoughts, that he hears all our words, and observes all our actions will preserve us from thinking any evil, from speaking any evil, and from doing any evil" (in *Phil. hom.* 8).

2. THE PRACTICE OF VIRTUE

As to the second effect, the practice of virtue, the presence of God is also a great means. Oh, what valor does a soldier exhibit in the presence of his sovereign! The sole thought that his prince by whom he shall be punished or rewarded is present inspires him with great courage and strength. Thus also when such a religious is in the presence of her Superior, with what exterior recollection does she pray, with what modesty and humility does she treat the sisters; with what care does she execute the directions that she receives! Hence if they reflected that God was looking at all their actions, all religious would do all things well, with a pure intention, without seeking to please any one but God, and without any regard to human respect. St. Basil says that were a person to find himself in the presence of a king and a peasant, his sole concern would be to please the king without any regard to the wishes of the peasant. Thus he that walks in the divine presence is regardless of the pleasure of creatures, and seeks only to please God, who sees him always.

3. TO UNITE THE SOUL WITH GOD

Finally, as to the third effect of the divine presence, that is, to unite the soul to God, it is an infallible rule that love is always increased by the presence of the object loved. This happens even among men, although the more they converse together, the more their defects are discovered. How much more shall the love of a soul for God increase if it keep him before its eyes! for the more it converses with him, the better it comprehends his beauty and amiableness. The morning and the evening meditation are not sufficient to keep the soul united with God. St. John Chrysostom says, that even water, if removed from the fire, soon returns to its natural temperature; and therefore after prayer it is necessary to preserve fervor by the presence of God, and by renewing our affections.

St. Bernard says of himself, that in the beginning of his conversion, when he found himself disturbed, or his fervor cooled, peace and the ardor of divine love were instantly restored by the remembrance of a deceased or absent saint (in *Cant.* s. 14). Now, how much greater the effect

116

which must be produced on a soul that loves God, by remembering that he is present, and that he is asking her love! David said that by the remembrance of his God he was filled with joy and consolation. *I remembered God, and was delighted* (Ps. 76:4). However great the affliction and desolation of a soul may be, if it loves God it will be consoled and freed from its affliction by remembering its beloved Lord. Hence, souls enamored of God live always with a tranquil heart and in continual peace; because, like the sunflower that always turns its face to the sun, they in all events and in all their actions seek always to live and act in the presence of God. "A true lover," says St. Teresa, "always remembers her beloved" (*Found.* ch. 5).

II

Practice of the Presence of God

LET us now come to the practice of this excellent exercise of the divine presence. This exercise consists partly in the operation of the under-standing, and partly in the operation of the will: of the understanding—in beholding God present; of the will—in uniting the soul to God, by acts of humiliation, of adoration, of love, and the like; of the latter we shall speak more particularly hereafter.

Of the Intellect

With regard to the intellect, the presence of God may be practiced in four ways:

1. IMAGINE CHRIST IS PRESENT

The first method is to imagine that our Redeemer, Jesus Christ, is present, that he is in our company, and that he sees us in whatsoever place we may be. We can at one time represent him in one mystery, and again in another: for example, now an infant lying in the manger of Bethlehem,

118

and again a pilgrim flying into Egypt; now a boy working in the shop of Nazareth, and again suffering as a criminal in his Passion in Jerusalem, scourged, or crowned with thorns, or nailed to a cross. St. Teresa (*Life* ch. 13) praises this method of practicing the presence of God. But it is necessary to remark, that though this method is good, it is not the best, nor is it always profitable: first, because it is not conformable to truth; for Jesus Christ, as God and man together, is present with us only after Communion, or when we are before the Blessed Sacrament. Besides, this mode is liable to illusion, or may at least injure the head by the efforts of the imagination. Hence, should you wish to practice it, you must do it sweetly, only when you find it useful, and without laboring to represent in the mind the peculiar features of our Savior, his countenance, his stature, or color. It is enough to represent him in a confused manner, as if he were observing all we do.

2. BEHOLDING WITH EYES OF FAITH

The second method, which is more secure and more excellent, is founded on the truth of faith, and consists in beholding with eyes of faith God present with us in every place, in considering that he encompasses us, that he sees and observes whatever we do. We indeed do not see him with the eyes of the flesh. Nor do we see the air, yet we know for certain that it surrounds us on every side, that we live in it; for without it we could neither breathe nor live. We do not see God, but our holy faith teaches that he is always present with us. *Do not I fill heaven and earth, says the Lord?* (Jer. 23:24). Is it not true, says God, that I fill heaven and earth by my presence? And as a sponge in the midst of the ocean is encompassed and saturated with water, so, says the Apostle, *we live in God, we move in God, and have our being in God* (Acts 17:28). And our God, says St. Augustine, observes every action, every word, every thought of each of us, as if he forgot all his other creatures, and had to attend only to us (*Solil.* c. 14; *Conf.* l. 3, c. 11). Hence, observing all we do, say, and think, he marks and registers all, in order to demand an account on the day of accounts, and to give us then the reward or the chastisement that we have deserved.

This second mode of practicing the divine presence does not fatigue the mind; for the exercise of it we need only enliven our faith with an affectionate act of the will, saying: My God, I believe firmly that You are here present. To this act we can easily add the acts of love, or of resignation, or of purity of intention, and the like.

3. RECOGNIZE HIM IN HIS CREATURES

The third means of preserving the remembrance of the presence of God is to recognize him in his creatures, which have from him their being, and their power of serving us. God is in the water to wash us, in the fire to warm us, in the sun to enlighten us, in food to nourish us, in clothes to cover us, and in like manner in all other things that he has created for our use. When we see a beautiful object, a beautiful garden, or a beautiful flower, let us think that there we behold a ray of the infinite beauty of God, who has given existence to that object. If we converse with a man of sanctity and learning, let us consider that it is God who imparts to him a small portion of his own holiness and wisdom. Thus, also, when we hear harmonious sounds, when we feel a fragrant odor, or taste delicious meat or drink, let us remember that God is the being who by his presence imparts to us these delights, that by them we may be induced to aspire to the eternal delights of paradise.

Let us accustom ourselves to behold in every object God, who presents himself to us in every creature; and let us offer him acts of thanksgiving and of love, remembering that from eternity he has thought of creating so many beautiful creatures that we might love him. St. Augustine says (*Enarr. in Ps.* 39): Learn to love your Creator in creatures; and fix not your affection on what God has made, lest you should become attached to creatures and lose him by whom you, too, have been created. This was the practice of the saint. At the sight of creatures he was accustomed to raise his heart to God; hence he exclaimed with love: Heaven and earth and all things tell me to love You (*Conf.* l. 10, c. 6). When he beheld the heavens, the stars, the fields, the mountains, he seemed to hear them say: Augustine, love God, for he has created you for no other end than that you might love him.

Thus, likewise, St. Teresa, when she beheld the plains, the sea, the rivers, or other beautiful creatures, felt as if they reproached her with ingratitude to God. Thus also St. Mary Magdalene de Pazzi, holding in her hand a flower or an apple, and looking at it, became enraptured with divine love, saying within herself: Then my God has thought from eternity of creating this fruit for my sake, and to give me a proof of the love that he bears me! It is also related of St. Simon Salo, that when in walking through the fields he saw flowers or herbs, he would strike them with his staff, saying: "Be silent! be silent! you reproach me with not loving that God who has made you so beautiful for my sake, that I might be induced to love him: I have already heard you; cease; reprove me no longer; be silent" (*Way of Perf.* ch. 29).

4. CONSIDER GOD WITHIN US

The fourth and most perfect means of remembering the divine presence is to consider God within us. We need not ascend to heaven to find our God; let us be recollected within ourselves, and in ourselves we shall find him. To treat in prayer with God as at a distance, causes great distraction. St. Teresa used to say: "I never knew how to make mental prayer as it ought to be made till God taught me this manner of praying: in this recollection within myself I have always found great profit."

To come to what is practical: It is necessary to know that God is present in us, in a manner different from that in which he is present in other creatures; in us he is present as in his own temple and his own house. *Know you not*, says the Apostle, *that you are the temple of God, and that the Spirit of God dwells in you?* (1 Cor. 3:16). Hence our Savior says, that into a soul that loves God, he comes with the Father and Holy Ghost, not to remain there for a short time, but to dwell in it forever, and there to establish an everlasting habitation. *If, any one love me, . . . my Father will*

123

love him, and we will come to him, and will make our abode with him (John 14:23).

The kings of the earth, though they have their great palaces, have, notwithstanding, their particular apartments in which they generally live. God is in all places; his presence fills heaven and earth; but he dwells in a particular manner in our souls, and there, as he himself tells us by the mouth of the Apostle, he delights to remain as in so many gardens of pleasure. *I will dwell in them, and will walk among them, and I will be their God* (2 Cor. 6:16). There he wishes us to love him and to pray to him: for he remains in us full of love and mercy, to hear our supplications, to receive our affections, to enlighten us, to govern us, to bestow on us his gifts, and to assist us in all that can contribute to our eternal salvation. Let us then often endeavor, on the one hand, to enliven our faith in this great truth, and annihilate ourselves at the sight of the great majesty that condescends to dwell within us; and on the other, let us be careful to make acts at one time of confidence, at another of oblation, and again of love of his infinite goodness; now thanking him for his favors, at another time rejoicing in his glory; and again asking counsel in our doubts; consoling ourselves always in the possession of this Sovereign Good within us, certain that no created power can deprive us of him, and that he will never depart from us unless we first voluntarily banish him from our hearts.

This was the little cell that St. Catherine of Sienna built within her heart, in which she lived always retired, always engaged in loving colloquies with God; thus she defended herself against the persecution of her parents, who had forbidden her to retire any more to her chamber for the purpose of praying. And in this little cell the saint made greater progress than she did by retiring to her room; for she was obliged to leave her chamber several times in the day. This interior cell she never left, but remained in it always recollected with God. Hence St. Teresa, speaking of the divine presence in our interior, said: "I believe that they who are able to lock themselves up in this little heaven in their souls, where he who created them is always present, walk in an excellent path, because they make great progress in a short time" (*Way of Perf.* ch. 29).

In a word, by this exercise of the presence of God the saints have succeeded in acquiring great treasures of merits. *I set the Lord always in my sight*, says the royal prophet, *for he is at my right hand that I be not moved* (Ps. 15:8). I endeavor to consider God always present, and observing all my actions. Blessed Henry Suso applied himself with so much attention to this holy exercise that he performed all his actions in the divine presence, and thus continually conversed with God by tender affections. St. Gertrude acquired the habit of this exercise so perfectly, that our Lord said of her to St. Mechtilde: "This beloved spouse always walks in my presence, seeking always to do my will, and directing all her works to my glory" (*Insin.* l. 1, c. 12). This was also the practice of St. Teresa; for in whatever occupation she found herself she never lost sight of her beloved Lord.

If, then, you ask me how often in the day you should remember the presence of God, I will answer you with St. Bernard (*De Int. Domo.* c. 27) that you ought to remember it every moment. As there is not a moment, says the saint, in which we do not enjoy the benefits of God, so there is not a moment in which we should not remember God, and prove our gratitude. If you knew that the king was always thinking of you and of your welfare, though he should confer no real benefit, still you could not remember his affection without feeling an interior love for him. It is certain that your God is always thinking of you, and that he incessantly confers favors on you at one time by his lights, at another by internal helps, and again by loving visits. Is it not ingratitude in you to be forgetful of him for any length of time? It is then a duty to endeavor to remember always, or at least as often as we can, the divine presence.

Practice of the Presence of God

This was the advice of the Lord to Abraham: *Walk before me, and be perfect* (Gen. 17:1). Endeavor to walk always in my presence, and you shall be perfect. Tobias gave the same advice to his son: *All the days of your life have God in your mind* (Tob. 4:6). My son, during your whole life keep God always before your eyes. The exercise of the divine presence St. Dorotheus recommended in a most special manner to his disciple, St. Dositheus, who besought him to tell him what he should do in order to be a saint: "Consider that God is always present, and that he is looking at you" (*Bolland. 23 Febr.*). St. Dorotheus relates that the good disciple was so faithful to the advice, that in all his occupations, and even in the severe infirmities with which he was visited, he never lost sight of God. Thus after being a soldier, and a dissolute young man, he attained in five years so high a degree of sanctity, that after death he was seen in heaven seated on a throne of glory equal to that of the most holy among the anchorets.

The great servant of God, Father Joseph Anchieta, who by the exercise of the divine presence arrived at such perfection, used to say that nothing else but our inattention to it can divert us from so holy an exercise. The prophet Micheas says: *I will show you, O man, what is good, and what the Lord requires of you, . . . to walk solicitous with your God* (Mich. 6:8). O man, I will

127

show you in what your welfare consists, and what the Lord demands of you; behold it: he wishes you to be solicitous, and that your whole concern be to do all your actions in his presence; because then all shall be well done. Hence, St. Gregory Nazianzen has written: "So often should we remember God as we draw breath" (*De Theol. orat.* 1). He adds, that by doing this we shall do all things. Another devout author says that meditation may in some cases be omitted; for example, in the time of sickness, or of important business, which cannot be deferred; but the exercise of the presence of God must be always practiced by acts of purity of intention, of oblation, and the like, as will be more fully explained hereafter.

Of the Will

Thus far, we have spoken of the operation of the intellect; allow me to speak of the application of the will to the holy exercise of the divine presence. And it is necessary, first, to know that to remain always before God, with the mind always fixed on him, is the happy lot of the saints; but in the present state it is morally impossible to keep up the presence of God without interruption. Hence we should endeavor to practice it to the best of our ability, not with a solicitous inquietude and indiscreet effort of the mind, but with sweetness and tranquility.

There are three means of facilitating the application of the will to this exercise.

1. FREQUENTLY RAISING THE HEART TO GOD

The first method consists in frequently raising the heart to God, by short but fervent ejaculations, or loving affections towards God, present with us. These may be practiced in all places and in all times, in walking, at work, at meals, and at recreation. These affections may be acts of election, of desire, of resignation, of oblation, of love, of renunciation, of thanksgiving, of petition, of humiliation, of confidence, and the like. In whatever occupation you find yourself, you can very easily turn to God from time to time and say, to him:

My God, I wish only for You, and nothing else.
I desire nothing but to be all Yours.
Dispose as You please of me, and of all that I possess.

I give myself entirely to You.
I love You more than myself.
I wish only what You wish.
I renounce all things for the love of You.
I thank You for the great graces You have
    bestowed upon me.
Assist me, have mercy on me.
Give me Your holy love.
Lord, I should be at this moment in hell.
I delight in Your felicity.
I would wish that all men loved You.
Do not permit me to be separated from You.
In You I place all my confidence.
When shall I see You and love You face to
    face?
Let all that I do and suffer be done and
    suffered for You. May Your holy will be
    always done!

The ancient Fathers set great value on all these
short prayers, by which we can practice the
presence of God more easily than by long prayers.
And St. John Chrysostom used to say, that he that
makes use of these short prayers or acts shuts the
door against the devil, and prevents him from
coming to molest him with bad thoughts (*De
Anna. Hom* 4).

Practice of the Presence of God

At certain special times it is necessary more particularly to enliven our faith in the divine presence. First, in the morning when we awake, by saying: My God, I believe that You are here present, and that You will be present with me in every place to which I shall go this day; watch over me, then, in all places, and do not permit me to offend You before Your divine eyes. Secondly, at the beginning of all our prayers, whether mental or vocal. The Venerable Cardinal Caracciolo, Bishop of Aversa, used to say, that he that makes mental prayer with distractions, shows that he has been negligent in making the act of faith in the presence of God. Thirdly, on occasion of any temptation against patience or chastity; for example, if you are seized with any sharp pain, or receive any grievous insult, or if any scandalous object be presented to you, instantly arm yourself with the divine presence, and excite your courage by remembering that God is looking at you. It was thus that David prepared himself to resist temptations. *My eyes are ever towards the Lord; for he shall pluck my feet out of the snare* (Ps. 24:15). I will keep my eyes on my God, and he will deliver me from the snares of my enemies. You must do the same when you have occasion to perform any very difficult act of virtue; you must imitate the valorous Judith, who, after having unsheathed the sword, and taken Holofernes, who was asleep, by the hair of the head, turned to God before she gave the stroke, and said: *Strengthen me, O Lord, in this hour* (Judith 13:9). Thus she courageously cut off his head.

2. THE INTENTION OF PLEASING GOD

The second method of preserving the presence of God by acts of the will is to renew always in distracting employments the intention of performing them all with the intention of pleasing God. And therefore, in the beginning of every action or occupation, whether you apply yourself to work, go to table, or to recreation, or to repose, say: Lord, I do not intend in this work my pleasure, but only the accomplishment of Your will. In the course of the action endeavor to renew your intention, saying: My God, may all be for Your glory. By these acts the presence of God is preserved without fatiguing the mind; for the very desire of pleasing God is a loving remembrance of his presence. It is also useful to fix certain times, or particular signs, in order to remember the divine presence; as when the clock strikes, when you look at the crucifix, when you enter or leave the cell. Some are accustomed to keep in their room some particular sign, to remind them of the presence of God.

3. RECOLLECT YOURSELF WITH GOD

The third method is, when you find yourself very much distracted during the day, and the mind oppressed with business, to procure leave from the Superior to retire, at least for a little, to the choir or to the cell, in order to recollect yourself with God. Were you on any day to feel bodily weakness, arising from excess of labor and long fasting, would you not take some refreshment in order to be able to proceed with the work? How much more careful should you be to treat the soul in a similar manner, when it begins to fail in courage, and to grow cold in divine love, in consequence of being a long time without food; that is, without prayer and recollection with God? I again repeat what Father Balthasar Alvarez used to say, that a soul out of prayer is like a fish out of water; the soul is, as it were, in a state of violence. Hence, after being a long time engaged in business and distracting occupations, a Christian should retire (if I may use the expression), to take breath in solitude, recollecting himself there with God, by affections and petitions. The life of bliss in heaven consists in seeing and loving God, and therefore I infer that the felicity of a soul on this earth consists also in loving and seeing God, not openly as in paradise, but with the eyes of faith, by which it beholds him always present with it; and thus acquires great reverence, confidence, and love towards its beloved Lord. He that lives in this manner, begins, even in this valley of tears, to live like the saints in heaven, who always see God. They *always see the face of my Father* (Matt 18:10), and therefore they cannot cease to love him. Thus he that lives in the divine presence will despise all earthly things, knowing that before God all is misery and smoke; and will begin in this life to possess that Sovereign Good who contents the heart more than all other goods.

PRAYER

My adored Jesus, You have not refused to give all Your blood for me; and shall I refuse to give You all my love? No, my beloved Redeemer, I offer myself entirely to You; accept me and dispose of me as You please. But since You give me the desire of Your pure love, teach me what I ought to do, and I will do it. Grant that this heart that was once miserably deprived of Your love may now neither love nor seek anything but You. Grant that my will may wish only what You wish. Unhappy me! I once, for the sake of my pleasures, despised Your will, and forgot You. Grant that from this day forward I may forget all things, even myself, to think only of loving and pleasing You. O my God, amiable above every good, how bitterly do I regret that up to now I have had so little regard for You! Lord, pardon me, draw me entirely to Yourself; do not permit me to love You but little, or to love anything but You. I hope for all things from Your goodness, and from Your merits, O my Jesus!

And I place all confidence in you, O my Queen, my advocate, and my Mother, Mary. Have pity on me, and recommend me to your Son, who hears your prayers, and refuses you nothing.

COLOPHON

"Talking with God" was transcribed, edited, and typeset by Scriptoria Books. Necessary corrections to the original text (including: misprints, punctuation, spelling, and citations) have been incorporated into this edition.

Original Sources

"The Way to Converse Always and Familiarly with God," in *The Way of Salvation and of Perfection*; St. Alphonsus Liguori, edited by Rev. Eugene Grimm, C.Ss.R, and published by Benziger Brothers, New York, and others.

"A Short Treatise on Prayer," in *The Way of Salvation and of Perfection*; St. Alphonsus Liguori, edited by Rev. Eugene Grimm, C.Ss.R, and published by Benziger Brothers, New York, and others.

"Mental Prayer," in *The Great Means of Salvation and of Perfection*; St. Alphonsus Liguori, edited by Rev. Eugene Grimm, C.Ss.R, and published by Benziger Brothers, New York, and others.

"The Presence of God," in *The True Spouse of Jesus Christ*; St. Alphonsus Liguori, edited by Rev. Eugene Grimm, C.Ss.R, and published by Benziger Brothers, New York, and others.

Book Data

Pages: 150
Binding: US Trade Paper
Trim Size: 5.25 x 8 inches; 13.35 x 20.32 centimeters
Interior: 60-pound white
Cover: 10 pt. C1S

For Legal Notices see Copyright page.

Made in the USA
Las Vegas, NV
04 April 2023

70134251R00085